HADRIAN'S WALL PATH

A Walk Through History

Paul Amess

Sam, the bravest man I know.

CONTENTS

Introduction
About the Wall

Hadrian's Wall had always fascinated me, including when I was a
mere whippersnapper. I remem-
ber being dragged up here as an uninterested child,
but quickly became incredibly interested indeed
when I found out that the Romans had built the
thing and that they used to murder people left,
right and centre. Now a UNESCO World Heritage
site since 1987, and with thousands of people
following the course of the Hadrian's Wall Walk
every year, especially since it was recognized as a
national trail in 2003, I wanted to find out a bit
about the history of the wall before I ventured
along it myself, and not only that, but the area in
general, and here is what I found out.

Running 73-miles from Bowness-on-Solway in the west, to Wallsend in the east, the
Romans had little choice other than to build the
wall because of those annoying Picts from the
north who were just damned right awkward in
that they refused to be conquered. Hadrian's biog-
rapher, Tacitus, specifically stated that *the wall
was to separate the Romans from the barbarians,*
which was a bit harsh, I reckon.

This was probably because, despite several

adventures in what is now modern-day Scotland, the Romans had never quite managed to pin down and control a people they referred to as savages, who fought naked while covered in blue paint, or possibly tattoos. The Romans even suspected that these people fought naked to show off their body decorations, but this is far from a fact. What is a fact, is that the Picts ran what we would today call an insurgency, and as we all know nowadays, not even the most powerful army in the world is necessarily going to win against a mass armed uprising of the people. Oh, the things we could learn from history, if only we bothered to.

It is important to add at this stage that we should not confuse the Picts with the Scots, as is a common mistake nowadays. I think the clearest way to demonstrate this is to remind ourselves that the last Pict King was killed in 843 AD, after which Kenneth Macalpin, the King of the Scots, decided to also crown himself as the new ruler of the Picts, thereby uniting them with the Scots. The Picts themselves had no choice on this at the time either, as Scotland was then also facing marauding Viking raiders. As the saying goes, the enemy of my enemy is my friend, with the common enemy being the Vikings. The latter were even more savage than the Picts.

Consequently, the Pictish language and culture gradually merged with that of the Scots, and today the language is no longer spoken by anyone. It should be said, however, that the Picts had a flourishing culture, at least until the Romans arrived, and left many beautiful carvings, pieces of art and jewellery to demonstrate their sophistication, so were not perhaps as savage as the Romans suggested. They just didn't like them.

Anyway, sick of their nasty neighbours and their uncivilized and quite frankly rude habits of popping over the border and stabbing to death a few of the Emperor's finest every now and then, things all changed when Emperor Hadrian came to power in 117 AD. Hadrian went on a tour of his empire, with the specific intention of strengthening its northern borders and consolidating the territories. Unlike any emperor before him, Hadrian had realized that the empire could not expand indefinitely, and therefore was intent on taking steps to ensure that stability and security would be the order of the day. He particularly wanted a visible border around the empire to deter others from invading, and this northern frontier would become the most telling sign of this strategy.

Possibly to the chants of *build that wall*, Hadrian visited Britain, or Britannia to give it its Roman name, in 122 AD, and construction started the same year. There is some speculation nowadays that another reason for the building of the wall was simply to occupy the troops that were stationed up here and building it would just give them something to do, which makes sense when you think about it.

Hadrian wasn't the first emperor to come

here though, that would be Julius Caesar almost two hundred years before, believe it or not, and that invasion almost never happened at all. The soldiers tasked with the occupation were not too happy about coming to the end of the world, as they called our humble little island. They even went on strike at one point, on the grounds that the place was infested with monsters, which should tell you something when you consider that men would rather mutiny than come up here. This invasion was only temporary though, as was the next one, once again by Caesar. It was only when Emperor Claudius popped over in 43 AD that the Roman presence became more permanent. The occupation would last almost 400 years, initially based around Colchester.

As a side note, Colchester became probably the most important Roman town in Britannia for a while, but in 60 AD, it was sacked by Boudicca, also known as Boadicea, which then made London, or Londinium, much more important. Boudicca had become enraged at the treatment of the indigenous people, but what really made her go postal was the brutal gang-rape of both of her daughters, which you could argue could have been somewhat anticipated. For this, she exacted a very harsh revenge indeed. When she sacked Colchester, she killed every man, woman and child without mercy. But for an accident of history, then, our capital could well have been Colchester to this very day.

Anyway, going back to the wall, it took 14 years to build it, and was built east to west, which is the opposite of the direction that most people choose to walk it today. The archaeologists know it was built east to west, as the size of the wall changes at various points. This was because it was taking too much manpower and stone to construct it, so the wall itself was narrowed from 10 feet wide to 8 feet wide pretty early on, and the foundations were changed too, though at a different time and place, but more of that later.

It was thought to be generally around 15 feet high and featured forts every five miles, milecastles every mile, obviously, with two turrets in between each of these, one every third of a mile. There were gates at regular intervals where people could cross from one side of the border, which it effectively became, to the other, although it is important to stress that the wall never marked the border between England and Scotland, despite popular misconceptions, as neither entity technically existed at the time. While milecastles were as advertised, every mile, we have to remember that this was Roman miles, not modern miles, and certainly not Robin miles, which I will explain later. At the time, a Roman mile was designated as being one thousand paces, but to be honest, this doesn't really help us, does it? It has since been agreed that a Roman mile is 0.92 modern miles, so there you go. Scientists have yet to agree on the definition of a Rob mile, however, although all agree that it is a bloody long way, and a lot longer than a normal mile, but again, more of that later.

As for what the wall looked like, this is still not known. Some historians think it was crenellated, and that soldiers would patrol the top of it. When you think about it, having a wall that you could not walk on would severely limit your tactical options, so while this is likely, it is definitely far from being certain, and the truth is nobody knows. It may have been painted too, with a lime-wash that would make it stand out strikingly against the dull landscape, but again this is just mere supposition, based on scant evidence. If it had been painted though, it would certainly have made it a bit more imposing, and would perhaps have made people think twice about messing with the Romans.

As a final point on Hadrian, it is believed that he never saw the wall that bears his name, which is a real shame. After leaving Britannia, he ventured around much of Europe and North Africa, but never again returned to this little island that sat at the extreme far north of the world's biggest empire.

The wall stood relatively unmolested for hundreds of years, even after the Romans left Britain and scarpered back to, well, Rome, I guess. This was because, at the time, us Britons were still running around wearing sacks and living in huts made from wood and mud, basically. Even the Venerable Bede, possibly the first historian of the English people, didn't know much about the wall and did not even know when it was built. However, when we discovered that we could build things out of stone and live in them instead and not have to worry about them burning down, well, all hell broke loose, and it was a bit of a free for all, resulting in some commendable recycling of the wall into houses, barns, churches and bridges, among many other things. Unfortunately, the result of all this pilfering means that there are large sections of the wall that are now, how shall I put it, purely hypothetical. The best bits of the wall are up in the hills in the middle of the country and presumably survive because it was just too hard for people to nick the stuff and cart it all the way back to town, for which we should be eternally grateful. So, with this in mind, let's do what we came here to do and start walking.

CHAPTER 1

Happy Campers

B ase camp was, appropriately enough, at Hadrian's Wall Camp Site, just a couple of miles outside of Haltwhistle. On previous walks, we had tended to move from campsite to campsite but seems as this walk was relatively short compared to, say, the Coast to Coast, we figured we could just drive to and from our start and finish points each day using a couple of vehicles. We would place one at our finish point, then drive to our start point and leave the other one there, and then use the other vehicle to collect this one at the end of the day. This saved the rigmarole of having to either use public transport or worse, packing up and moving campsites every day or so. There was just one teeny, tiny problem, though. The two vehicles we had were one car and one van, and the van only had three seats, so we would have to take turns going in the back and rolling around for a while, and hoping we don't get stopped by the rozzers.

We had chosen well with this campsite

though. As well as being run by a very friendly husband and wife team who had all the time in the world when it came to talking to us, it also had excellent shower and washing facilities, but most importantly, it had the world's oldest cat. I am being entirely serious. This thing looked ancient, and it had a chunk missing from one of its ears which clearly indicated a story to tell there, and its fur reminded me of an antique rug that had lost much of its body to moths over the years. I think it was deaf, too, as it never moved when you went near it, and one day, just as I was beginning to wonder if it was actually dead, I saw it blink, which is about the only movement I witnessed from it over the whole week we were there.

The owners, of the campsite and presumably the cat also, Steve and Tracy, said they had just bought the campsite as part of their mid-life crisis, and to be honest, it's definitely better than buying a motorbike or having hair implants. They had inherited the cat, which made sense, as it was a bit like one of those ugly pets that always seem to be left behind at animal sanctuaries. You know the ones I mean, teeth missing, cross-eyed, that sort of thing. They had decided to turn their backs on their commute to work, and have instead devoted themselves to this place which is clearly very important to both of them. As they tell me this, I am finding myself feeling a bit jealous, but in a good way, for there is nothing I would love to do more than to do the same thing. Buy a pad in the country, and spend the time whiling away the hours cleaning toilets and showers after messy campers. Okay, maybe not that bit, but the country thing definitely.

Anyway, they put us right at the back of the campsite, which was more our request really, as this way we will be away from all the noisy people, and particularly any children. Plus, it means we get to make as much noise as we want to make, just in case. We don't usually have parties or anything like that, but we do sometimes talk well into the night, and wouldn't want to annoy anybody.

Unfortunately, the back of the campsite is up something of a steep hill, and although there is a track, it proves somewhat challenging to get the van up there. This is a problem, as all of our gear is in the van and we don't really want to be carting everything up there by hand. The first time Chris tried to drive the van up, he didn't even get a third of the way and had to slowly reverse down and start again. He got a bit more of a run up on his second attempt but still failed to get to the top, which only made us more certain that we would soon be doing a heck of a lot of lifting. On the third attempt, though, luck was on our side, and despite a few wheel spins and some squeaky moments, up to the top the van went, skidding gracefully to a halt in just the right place. We waited for a few seconds to see if it was just going to slide down the steep grass slope, and when we figured this was probably not going to happen, we put some chocks under the wheels and started to unpack.

Chris always took his van camping, as we could chuck all of our gear into it, which meant that our cars would not be ridiculously over-loaded. I do laugh when you see these cars flying along the motorway at 70 miles per hour which are absolutely crammed to the rafters with tents, sleeping bags and pillows, often with bikes and ca-noes on the roof. Occasionally, we are even treated to the hilarious sight of kids' faces squashed up against back windows, pushed there by bags of clothes and buckets and spades and packs of saus-ages, and I often wonder how they manage to get enough oxygen. Not for us though, as we are civil-ized travellers, and anyway we don't take any kids with us.

I have already introduced Chris, but I will tell you a couple of other things about him. Chris is not very tall, but do not let that fool you. He should not be messed with, as he does not take too kindly to this; oh, and don't feed him after mid-night. He will do anything to help anyone, how-ever, and he often does, and I have said before that he is possibly the most generous person I know, which is a statement I will stick to, although I mean apart from myself of course. I have been going walking with Chris for years, and he is like a mountain goat. When he sees a hill, he is gone, often leaving the rest of us behind as we struggle up it in our snail-like manner. Oh, and he always, absolutely always, brings Haribos on every walk, usually the sour ones, so we always try to stay close by.

Robin, who usually has the map and can generally be found up front, is somewhat taller than Chris, or me, or most people that I know for that matter, so people tend not to mess with him either. However, he is not in any way scary and can even be described as a gentle giant. He too would help anyone with more or less anything, so long as it was legal anyway, and he often has. He does, however, have one fatal flaw. Perhaps because of his size, he does tend to miss pages out of map books and guide books, maybe because he struggles with the tiny pages in his giant hands. That this results in extra mileage for us mere mortals has become almost the norm, so whenever we talk of how many miles a walk may be, we go to great lengths to differentiate between statute miles, and Rob miles, which we mentioned earlier. We have calculated, through years of careful measurements and calibration, that a Rob mile is actually equal to exactly 1.25 statute miles. This means that if Rob tells us that today we will be walking 12 miles, we simply times it by 1.25 to give us the true figure of today's walk, which would, in fact, be 15 miles. Simples.

There is also a new member of our motley crew. Anthony had been out with us once or twice on a couple of short walks, and he was quite a likeable guy. Like us, he was down to earth and friendly and fitted right in straight away. He enjoyed the odd beer, and in the limited number of times I had met him, I found he was very pleasant to talk to. He had a couple of children and had even brought his daughter along on one of our walks, which had really surprised me, as my own children had laughed in ridicule when I had suggested something similar to them.

So that is the gang, and for the next few days, we will be making our way across the north of England, West to East, following the course of Hadrian's Wall Walk, which will be a first for all of us. We had all been up to this part of the country at one time or another, and I know that I, for one, had walked along some very small parts of the wall, but none of us had ever done the full walk, so it should be at least some kind of adventure for us all, and for you too, hopefully.

There are a couple of people notable for their absence in our little group, though. On some, or most actually, of our previous walks, we had also been accompanied by Andy and Rob, although I mean a different Rob of course. Unfortunately, neither could be here today, as Andy was busy changing nappies on his latest offspring, and Rob was sunning it in Jamaica, the fool. Both had expressed regret at not being able to join us this week; however, I suspect Rob was somewhat taking the mick. I had already received a couple of text messages from him informing me of the current temperature in Montego Bay - 32 degrees

Celsius - as well as a lurid description of his latest cocktail - sex on the beach - and knowing him as I do, I suspected this was probably going to continue for the next few days, either until he came home, or until I flew over there and did him in.

Anyway, between the four of us, we soon had the tents nicely set up on the top of our little hill. We had been watched as we did this by some pigs in the next field, who seemed very interested in our supplies, though I didn't think they had any chance of getting through the fence.

After pumping up our airbeds and chucking everything else in, we decided it was time to head into Haltwhistle for some food. Haltwhistle is somewhat familiar to me, in that I have been here once or twice over the last few years. One of its claims to fame is that it lies at the centre of Britain, although this is certainly debatable. The nice people from the Ordnance Survey have measured this, and they have figured out that the actual centre of Britain lies either here, or possibly at Dunsop Bridge in Lancashire, which is worryingly around seventy miles due south of here, suggesting that there is certainly some room for interpretation at least.

I wasn't exactly sure what method they used to figure this out, but when I read about it, it didn't sound altogether scientific, it has to be said. Apparently, if you use a pair of scissors to cut out the whole of the United Kingdom, and balance it on a church spire, voila, Haltwhistle is the balance point. They go on to make this sound more scientific than it actually is by giving it a fancy name, which is the gravitational method, but you can call it whatever you want, though this will not make it science, ever. If I had suggested this in my science class at school, what do you think the reaction would have been? Exactly. A week of detention.

Still, there are a whole host of other criteria which also suggest that the true centre of Britain is in fact right here, although most of them have been suggested by none other than the manager of the local hotel, Dave Taylor, who runs, not surprisingly, The Centre of Britain Hotel, slap bang in the middle of town obviously. It's a clever marketing ploy, however, and it is somewhat successful, so in the absence of a better contender, of which Dunsop Bridge certainly is not, I am going to go with the flow and concede to Haltwhistle on this one.

We arrive in town fairly late on, and I can't figure out if the place is just coming to life or just going to sleep. It is very nice and picturesque, but there is not a lot of choice of places to eat; however, we end up at the Black Bull, where we all enjoy a fine meal. I had the steak and ale pie, and wash it down with a quick beer. Chatting excitedly about our upcoming walk, we check the weather forecast which tells us that there is a fifty per cent chance of rain for the next couple of days, which is not exactly helpful when you think about it. Before long, we are on our way back to the campsite to tuck ourselves in for an early night and an early morning, where hopefully we will all wake up after a refreshing night's sleep and with a spring in our step, ready to tackle day one of our epic walk.

CHAPTER 2

Bowness to Linstock

The following morning, we all drag ourselves out of our tents still half asleep and not exactly rearing to go. Perhaps unwisely, we had opened some beers when we got back to camp the night before and had sat under the stars chatting for quite some time. It wasn't so much the beers, as we only had a couple each, but it was the lateness of the night that was perhaps the problem. We had certainly carried on talking well into the early hours, which is perhaps not advisable when you have a pretty long walk to do the following day. I had soon gone to sleep though, but had a strange nightmare about a zombie cat, and when I woke up in the early hours, I made a point of making sure the tent was zipped up properly.

The good news though was that it wasn't raining, although there was certainly a lot of cloud hanging around. The campsite was in the Tyne Valley, so would be subject to a different weather pattern to where we were heading anyway, so we had no choice other than to see what happened when we jumped in the car a little later on.

Doing our usual thing with breakfast, which is all chipping in to help cook, clean and wash up, we were soon ready to head off on our first day's adventure. The plan today was to leave the van at a car park in the small village of Linstock just east of Carlisle and around a mile from the motorway. We would then drive to Bowness-on-Solway, where we would begin our long walk back to Linstock. We would start off by following the road through Port Carlisle towards Drumburgh and then Burgh-by-Sands. Next, we would join the River Eden for a bit, all the way through Carlisle, where we would cross over the river and into Rickerby Park, through the village of the same name, and then follow a minor road over the motorway into Linstock and back to Chris' van. A short hop back to Bowness to get the car would complete day one, after which we would probably saw off our feet and buy new ones. This route sounded simple and pretty easy and was not at all hilly, and I, for one, was looking forward to it.

The drive to Bowness took longer than expected, being around sixty miles on mostly minor roads and including, of course, the stop at Linstock to drop Chris' van off. We continued on to Bowness in the car and seemed to go in a roundabout manner, but soon enough we saw the sea, which meant we were at our destination.

Bowness was a pretty but compact little place, with equally compact little streets. There were not that many places to park, though we did find a small car park at the western end of the village, however, it was full. We got out of the car anyway, just to have a look around, as this was such a beautiful spot, but we also wanted to see if there was anywhere else nearby to leave the car.

Just to the west of the village, we could see a spit of land sticking out into the Solway estuary. I knew what this was, I thought to myself, and told the story to the others, promising them it was interesting. This is, in fact, what remains of a railway bridge that used to cross from here to Scotland, and at over a mile long, was the longest in the country for its time. If you look carefully or have binoculars, it is possible to make out a similar spot on the opposite bank too, which is of course in Scotland itself.

This was Solway Junction Railway and was built by those ever so industrious Victorians in the late 1860s, and it both shortened the journey time to Scotland and meant that trains could avoid the busy lines of Carlisle. It ran into problems very soon, though, when it was severely damaged by ice build-up in the waters below, which must have been at a time when winters were actually cold.

The winters of both 1874 and 1881 were, in fact, particularly chilly, and parts of the River Esk, as well as the River Eden, froze over. As they thawed, mini-icebergs broke off and severely damaged the bridge on both occasions, with the 1881 thaw destroying almost a third of the bridge alone.

It was rebuilt, though, and went on to serve both passengers and freight for some time after that. By 1914, however, passenger services had ceased, and its use was discontinued altogether after 1921, after which it fell into disuse and disrepair. This is, perhaps, where the story gets interesting.

I say disuse, but on second thoughts, this is probably not quite the right word. It was still used, just not by trains. At this time, the drinking laws in England and Scotland were much more varied than they are now. In Scotland, for instance, it was forbidden to buy alcohol on the sabbath, so every Sunday, you would see dozens of Scots merrily making their way across the bridge on foot, intent on taking advantage of our more liberal rules here in England. Unfortunately, these drunken Scots were even merrier on their way home late on a Sunday night or early on a Mondy morning, and it became quite common for them to fall off the bridge and into the waters below, never to be seen again. This became such a problem, that in 1934 the powers that be decided enough was enough, and promptly demolished the bridge, thereby ending the illicit cross border booze trips immediately, and putting to an end any and all late-night swimming.

We looked around the area next to the car park and considered leaving the car on a grass verge, though decided against it as the road was pretty narrow here, so we jumped back into the car and slowly drove into the village. We probably looked a bit shifty, four blokes in a car proceeding slowly along through the streets at crawling speed while having a good look all around us. More than a couple of people gave us a suspicious look, and I don't blame them one bit.

We did not find anywhere else to park in the village, and soon ended up right on the other side, where Anthony left his car at a point where the houses stopped, and a long straight road began. A sign announced the possibility of tidal flooding, but Anthony didn't seem too concerned, and anyway, he said he had insurance. As we headed back into the village to find the starting point of the walk, I seriously wondered if that car would still be there in 12 hours, after the tide had been in and gone out again, but reckoned that it could do with a bit of a wash anyway.

Wandering through the village, we quickly found a small shop and café, where we decided to grab a quick drink and use the facilities. It looked like an old farm, and some enterprising individual had decided to capitalize on all us rich walkers and try to fleece us for a few pounds. A small log cabin did the trick, doubling up as the café, and there was also a nice outdoor seating area with plenty of benches, one of which we appropriated for our own use. The toilets were through the main building and out the back, and when I went, I had to dodge several friendly chickens who perhaps mistook my toes for food. Unfortunately, wherever you get chickens, you get chicken poop, and I found myself really wishing I had left my shoes on. I was pleasantly surprised when in the back I found several what can only be described as gipsy style caravan holiday homes, and very nice they were too.

We talked to the guy that ran this little enterprise, and he told us of his holiday cottages, his motorhomes and his bed and breakfast that he also ran, leaving us somewhat gobsmacked. That was not all though, as he also did evening meals, he told us, which we instantly thought might solve our problem of where to eat that night. Taking his number, he directed us to the start of the walk, and he told us he would see us later in the day. He was certainly confident that one, and a further demonstration of his industriousness was a sign that announced his ice cream shop – for dogs! He did not let us leave, though, until we purchased a rather expensive Hadrian's Wall Passport. The idea of this is to get it stamped at key points along the route, either to prove to your disbelieving wife that you have spent the week walking and not sitting in a pub, or just to keep as a memento. We did not mind, though, as the money all goes to good causes.

Lastly, this local Richard Branson had also

paid for and erected a sign telling the story of Gaius Ulpus Sabinus, who was a Roman Legionnaire around here some two millennia ago. The sign also told us that the Roman name for Bowness was Maia, which I was not sure how to pronounce, and that being the westernmost point of the wall, there had been a pretty big fort here.

We wandered through the streets and through a little snicket down to the shore, where we found ourselves on the southern bank of the Solway Firth. A small but impressive pavilion marks the official start of the Hadrian's Wall Walk, and of course, we did the touristy thing of taking each other's picture as well as our own, and this is where we also got the first stamp in our nice expensive passports.

A sign here tells us that Wallsend is 84 miles away along with a note wishing all walkers good luck, and with that, we are off. No sooner than we set off though, we come across a wall full of dead boots that have been repurposed as plant pots, presumably from dead hikers that have done the walk the other way around and not from people who started here and immediately gave up, but you never know.

We follow the path along the shoreline for a short while, and then pass through a little gate and find ourselves back at Anthony's car. Resisting the temptation to get back in it and drive straight to the nearest pub, we plod on westwards and past the sign that proclaims the possibility of flooding.

There are some small bungalows here that are ridiculously close to the shoreline and not all that high, and I suspect at some point that they have probably been flooded, although there is no one around to ask.

The road is long and straight, something that we will presumably get used to along what are essentially Roman roads, and after a couple of miles, we meet an elderly couple who are clearly twitchers. They excitedly tell us of how they have, that very day, seen hen harriers, willow tits, and a lesser spotted gob-shite, bless them. Unfortunately, I've seen nothing of the such, and I didn't even see the dog muck that I stepped in half a mile back, although I figured it would be well gone by the time we finished walking.

We pass signs telling us variously that floodwaters get to this point, that here the water will be two feet deep when flooded, and that if you want to go beyond this point, you really need some arm-bands, just in case. Undaunted, and being the brave sorts that we are, we carry on regardless and eventually arrive at Port Carlisle and all the excitement that it offers. A few nice houses dot our right, but other than that we feel a bit let down by the place as we turn off the road and to the left, which leads us through a gate and down a track.

Almost immediately, we encounter an older gentleman with a sign similar to the one you see at Land's End and John o' Groats. He has a box of letters and numbers and immediately engages us in a friendly but firm manner, enquiring how far we have come, how far we are going, and how much money we have in our pockets. He is a mine of information, and tells us that the village used to be called Fishers Cross, but had its name changed to Port Carlisle to make it sound good. I can see what is going on with this one, I immediately think. He offers to put the name of our home city of Hull on the sign for a photo opportunity and insists that we don't have to pay, but if we wish to make a donation, well, that is something altogether different. We duly oblige him, and do our little photo thing, and then Robin stuffs a crispy fresh banknote in his donation box. Well, that is the least we could do seems as he had been so polite whilst he was fleecing us.

We carried on our merry way, secretly quite chuffed about this little bit of blatant tourism so early on the walk, and hoped for lots more little interactions just like it. We had the Solway Firth on our left, with sweeping views north towards Scotland, and it was all very pleasing to the eye on what was turning into a very fine day, although we had seen no sign of the wall as yet.

We soon came across the old harbour wall of Port Carlisle, which now stood as an island a few hundred feet from the shore, and I wondered if it was accessible at low tide. I would have loved to have gone to have a look, but there was no chance today. We were now on the disused railway line which led from Bowness to Carlisle. This little bit of track has an interesting history, and in fact, started life as a canal. Indeed, if you look carefully at the shoreline here, just where the bridge crosses a small stream, it is possible to see where the canal met the sea. All the stonework is still there for what was once, though very briefly, the sea lock. When technology improved and faster links were needed, some industrious entrepreneurs promptly filled the canal in and built a railway line where boats had once sailed, speeding up connection times considerably. This allowed for the area to flourish and for a lot of people to get very rich, very quickly.

After a while, the path took us into scrubland where midges prevailed, and we were glad when we crossed the road and found ourselves in more hospitable surroundings. Passing a small caravan park, we wandered along a narrow lane hemmed in on either side by lush ferns, dodging puddles left by the rain earlier.

We soon found ourselves in Glasson, where we made use of the picnic tables opposite the Highland Laddie Inn for a minute or two, just to tighten shoelaces and get some sweets from Rob's backpack. Jelly Babies were the flavour of the day and were soon devoured by all. A little further on, I spied a bus stop that was built of sturdy stone and wondered if the stones had been taken from a certain wall, though I ultimately decided probably not.

A left turn led us into a field full of freshly shaved sheep, who bleated about our presence and ran away as fast as they could. The path turned into a track and after a half a mile or so, a left turn took us into Drumburgh, with still no sight of the wall.

I say no sight of the wall, but technically we could see a bit of it, but it was no longer a wall. As we left the village, there is a large and impressive house on the right, which is actually Drumburgh Castle. This is a Peel Tower, which is basically a heavily fortified house, and this one looks very fortified indeed. The front door is on the first floor up an impressive flight of steps, which would have enabled anyone who lived there to easily slay their enemies with a hail of arrows and some boiling oil as they approached, something which today could be applied to cold callers selling double glazing or solar panels or time-shares in Uzbekistan and the like. I have one of those little stickers stuck in my window which says strictly no cold-callers and which nobody takes a blind bit of notice of, and quite frankly, I would love to see them ignore a hail of arrows and some boiling oil. And if you're wondering what my problem is with Uzbekistan, there isn't one; it's the people selling timeshares I have a problem with.

The road now dropped a little, down a shallow hill, and went dead straight, disappearing into the distance. Cows wandered freely, and various signs warned again of the dangers of flooding on this stretch of road, which was worrying as the tide was definitely coming in. It is here that we got our first hint of what was once a part of the larger wall structure, which was the vallum. The vallum was basically a ditch 10 feet deep and 20 feet wide with mounds on either side which was built to the south of the wall and is thought to have marked the boundary of the military area, where civilians were not permitted, presumably suffering a hail of arrows and some boiling oil if they ventured across. It ran the full length of the wall, and was sometimes carved through solid rock, but was distinctly separate from the wall though probably built at around the same time or shortly after, as it deviates around some of the forts that were built with the wall itself.

This is quite a straight stretch of road, as I have already said, which meant that some of the traffic passing us was doing so at quite some speed, which was a bit unnerving. We kept having to jump onto the verge, which although was ample, was also pretty boggy and meant the possibility of wet feet, but was better than a trip to the hospital, I guess. For a while, I walked on top of the mound instead but came back on the road at a sign that pointed to Finglandrigg, a most odd name. The mound was nothing to do with the wall, by the way, but was just a part of the modern-day flood defences.

The road continued eastwards as straight as ever, and as we all know these Romans were very good at that, and to our right was the route of the old canal and of course, the railway. When they had turned one into the other, they also had to mess with all of the bridges to increase the height, as they were not quite high enough for steam engines, which must have been a bit of a faff, I thought. If you look carefully, you can also see where ropes from the canal boats have marked the top of the bridges underneath and made the stone smooth and round.

We passed the villages of Bousted Hill, which was indeed built on a hill, probably to the eternal gratitude of the people that live there and hopefully never gets flooded, and approached Longburgh, which looked like it wasn't so much on a hill but did have some very nice houses.

We were nearly at our first stopping point, which was Burgh-by-Sands, where we hoped to stop for some lunch at the pub, but getting here had seemed to have taken a lot longer than it had looked like it would on the map. I presumed it was because the road was so straight and featureless and had maybe made the walk seem longer than it actually was, but regardless, we were all ready for a rest.

Passing Longburgh, we left the Solway Firth behind and now had views of fields and trees instead, which of course would remain with us for the next 80 miles or so until we arrived at the other side of the country. We passed a group of walkers going the other way and enquired if they too were doing the full walk, but they looked at us as if we were mad and said they were locals and were just doing a short circuit.

As we entered Burgh-by-Sands, I wondered where the sands were, as we now clearly seemed to be miles from the sea. A road sign announced a new speed limit of 30 miles per hour, something that the next few passing motorists had clearly missed, probably because they were moving faster than light, so as we entered the village proper, we took advantage of the footpaths. The walk was definitely well signposted, although this wasn't necessary at the moment as the route was more or less completely straightforward, but at least we knew we weren't lost, well not yet anyway. Rounding a couple of bends past some nicely kept gardens, we eventually found ourselves at the other end of this extremely long village, but more importantly at the Greyhound Inn.

Unfortunately, and quite disastrously, the pub was closed, but we stopped anyway and took advantage of the picnic tables where we ate our sandwiches and whatnot. It was still quite a pleasant day, but a few wasps annoyed us by buzzing around our heads while we ate. This was probably Chris' fault, as he had peeled a big juicy orange near the bin, and he had then cunningly lured them back to our table.

There was a statue next to the pub, and I went over to have a look. It was quite impressive, showing a man holding a crown and brandishing a vicious looking sword. I had no idea who this was as I did not recognize the face, but luckily a sign informed me that it was King Edward I. The sign proclaimed that he died here in 1307 while fighting Robert the Bruce and was laid in nearby St Michael's church. I always enjoy a quick, childish chuckle when I find out where some local dignitary got laid, but then I'm just a big daft kid.

I'm sure you will have heard of Edward I, who was also known as Edward Longshanks and even the Hammer of the Scots, although he didn't get this latter nickname until well after his death. The Longshanks name comes from the fact that he was ridiculously tall at 6 feet 2 inches when at the time, most people were a good four feet shorter than this. They weren't of course, I'm just playing with you, but people were generally a lot shorter than him anyway. The Hammer of the Scots is probably self-explanatory, but, spoiler alert, Eddie was a bit of a xenophobe. It wasn't just the Scots he upset you see. He had a particularly good go at the Welsh, and in a fit of rage, he even expelled all Jews from England in 1290, so I suspect there was a considerable bit of partying in 1307 when he finally shuffled off this mortal coil not far from this very spot.

The sign telling of his death does not tell the full story, however. The inference when you read it is that he perhaps died in battle, on his way to meet Robert the Bruce and all that, but the truth is quite the opposite. Edward had been ill and was suffering from dysentery, and in July 1307 he was heading north to fight Robert the Bruce. He had already caught and killed William Wallace in 1305, and if you've ever seen *Braveheart*, you might already know that. His health declined rapidly though, and he could only ride 2 miles a day, and it was at Burgh-by-Sands that he was forced to stop completely. On the 7th July, when his servants helped him out of bed, he expediently expired right in their arms, and that was that. He did lay in the local church for a while as has already been said but was then taken back to London and buried in Westminster Abbey. Bitter to the end, he asked for his bones to be carried into battle against the Scots, but no one could be bothered, so in Westminster he remained. Some have said, regarding his Hammer of the Scots nickname, that it actually turns out that it was the anvil that wore down the hammer, which is a bit poetic and which I kind of like.

His tomb was opened in 1774, bizarrely just so that they could measure his height, and his body was found to be surprisingly well preserved. It was only when they re-opened it and saw the inscription that read *Here is Edward I, Hammer of the Scots, 1308. Keep the Vow* that his new nickname became really popular, and since then, it has well and truly stuck.

As we ate, a couple of other walkers turned up and were as disappointed as us to find the pub shut, especially as it was the first opportunity for refreshment since starting at Bowness. We chatted to them and found out they were from Italy and were doing the full walk over what would be a leisurely week or so, although they were staying in nice posh hotels as opposed to camping like us plebs. They asked us if we knew where the next pub or café was, but we obviously didn't have a clue, however, suggested that as Carlisle was just a few miles away, there would be ample refreshment there.

They wandered off a couple of minutes later, thankfully batting their heads with their hands as they kindly escorted our wasps away, and we soon followed, walking along the edge of the playing field for a while so as to keep away from the road. I had thought we had already arrived at the other end of the village, but I was wrong, and we passed a good few houses before we came to the true end. We came to St Michael's Church, which was, of course, the temporary resting place of the corpse of Edward I, and decided to pop in for a look. I mean, if it's good enough for a king, it's good enough for us.

A leaflet tells us that the church is built on the site of a Roman fort called Aballava or Alacazam or Abracadabra or something like that, and is in fact, like so many buildings we will encounter, built from the stones of the wall itself. The walls are quite thick, and there are steps in the west wall that lead to a secret chamber, which was cool, though no matter what I pressed and pulled and pushed, nothing opened. The stained-glass windows were particularly striking, especially the one depicting Edward I.

Cooler still, is the village's possible though somewhat more tenuous link, to none other than King Arthur. This is said to be the possible location of the mythical Avalon, which does sound a bit like Aballava, it has to be said, and could, in fact, be the very place where King Arthur died and where the famous sword Excalibur was forged. True or not, it is a fascinating story.

Leaving Arthur behind, the walk out of the village led us on a narrow road with high hedges, but with very little in the way of grass verge, so it was stop and start every time a car or truck came along. Luckily it was only a few hundred feet before we came to a lay-by where we turned off the road and onto a path. After a short dash north, we found ourselves heading east on the course of the wall itself, although once again there was absolutely no sign of what had once stood here.

It was, however, a very pleasant walk through fields, initially following a line of trees where we shared the space with lots of cows. This soon turned into a well-worn track, and before long, we were in Beaumont.

A sign took us left at the village green, down towards the River Eden, but after a few hundred feet we encountered another sign that said the path had been temporarily diverted due to ongoing works with the path, so we had to go back to the green and start again.

We bumped into the Italians again, who were coming the other way and who looked as puzzled as us. Although the diversion was clearly stated as being in place, the alternative route was far from clear, so outside of St Mary's church, which was built on a pretty little hill, we put our heads together and figured that we still didn't know the right way to go. Looking at the map though, it would be possible to follow a minor road south-east which would bring us back on track, which is just what we did, followed by the Italians who had thoughtfully given us back our wasps.

After a couple of miles, we started to see signs of houses on our left, which marked the beginning of Kirkandrews-on-Eden. We passed what looked like a village hall, and when we got to a small cemetery, we took a left which finally led us back onto the path, though strangely we saw no sign of a church. A short hop across some fields then saw us arrive at Grinsdale, which is where the path began to follow the banks of the River Eden. There were some cows here that had their back legs shackled together, and although there is probably a sensible reason for this, such as to stop the cows murdering passing city softies, it was not a good look, and I found myself feeling a bit sorry for them, the big sentimental fool that I am.

It was a pleasure, however, to wander along the riverbank, which offered the third stage of today's walk. First had been the long trudge along the Solway Firth, which although it had been interesting, we had welcomed the change of scenery to fields somewhere near Longburgh. I think I speak for us all when I say we now welcomed another change of scenery to riverbank, as it just creates a bit of variety in things to look at along the way.

As we walked along, we followed a gradual but definite bend to the left, passing under a canopy of trees that created yet more variety in our route. Although there were more than a few ups and downs, and the odd scramble, we very much enjoyed this bit of the walk. We met few people initially, but as we drew nearer to Carlisle, we did encounter the odd dog walker along with a rather amorous couple walking hand in hand and smooching as they went. A couple of times, the path went away from the river briefly, at one point taking us through a field full of cows who refused to get out of the way.

These cows were the traditional black and white cow we usually see in Britain and are called Holstein-Friesians. If you ask almost anyone, anywhere, to draw a cow, this is probably what you will get, although if you ask me, you probably won't recognize my efforts, that bad am I at drawing. Anyway, they are common for a reason though, and that is because they generally give the most milk, so it makes economic sense for farmers to have loads of them. They are normally docile and just stare at you, but I think these were a bit over-friendly and wanted a bit of a cuddle. As we made our way through the herd, then, I made sure I was in the middle of our little group, and might at least be the last to die should anything go wrong.

We somehow survived and ended up back in the woods, and after passing under a couple of bridges, we found ourselves on the outskirts of Carlisle and next to some playing fields where it looked like there was some sort of sports tournament going on. An ice-cream van at the other side of the field beckoned us but proved to be too far out of our way, so we carried on into town. I might have been tempted, but I was once traumatized as a child when I was run over by an ice cream van when I was about 4 years old. It wasn't actually that bad as I recall, and I think I got free ice creams for a couple of years. This was even better than it sounds because it was a Mr Whippy ice cream van, and not that rubbish that you scoop out of a tub.

It was a thoroughly pleasant walk into the city, and you would never guess that the place is cursed. I kid you not, it is actually cursed, and right up to the modern-day, this curse is ongoing and has even forced local politicians to get involved, knowledge which force me to question whether or not I really was in the 21st century.

Around 500 years ago, a guy called Gavin Dunbar, the Archbishop of Glasgow, had seemingly reached the limits of his patience with the cross border Reiver people, who were constantly pillaging anything and everything that they could get away with. He decided to write a curse, and this wasn't just a quick one-liner such as *may your days be long and your nights lonely*, oh no, he went to town on this one.

After presumably necking a barrel or two of Glasgow's best mead, Dunbar came up with a doozy of a curse, which, at 1,069 words, was surprisingly quite specific.

I curse their head and all the hairs on their head. I curse their face, their brain, their mouth, their tongue, their teeth. May the thunder and lightning which rained down upon Sodom and Gomorrah, rain down upon them.

And that wasn't even the half of it. He cursed them within and without, sitting and standing, coming and going. He cursed their parents, their children, their brothers and their sisters. He even cursed their sheep, their geese, and, quite bizarrely, their cabbages. He cursed them to drown and to burn, though presumably not at the same time, and he cursed plagues upon them for all eternity. He did not, however, curse the local football team, but more of that later.

Apparently, it worked, though, and that was the end of the Reiver people. Fast forward a few hundred years, and to 2001, when some bright spark at the council asked Gordon Young, a local artist, to carve 383 words of the curse onto a stone, for what purpose I have no idea.

Since then, a series of unfortunate events

has hit the city. Foot and mouth disease came immediately, probably while Young was still holding his chisel, followed by floods in 2005 when the River Eden burst its banks and placed a large part of the city under several feet of water. The local football club was relegated, a large bakery burned down and there were multiple job losses in the city, all after the commissioning of the stupid curse stone. Like I said earlier though, Archbishop Dunbar did not curse the local football team, so I am afraid that is all on them.

Luckily, though, a local politician, with clearly nothing better to do such as revitalize the local economy or improve environmental conditions for the local people, has taken up the cause and is campaigning for the stone to be removed, or better still, smashed to smithereens. Gordon Young, however, who of course created the stone, has likened the local council to the Taliban, who infamously smashed up some giant Buddha statues in Afghanistan in 2001. Attempts were even made to ask the modern-day Archbishop of Glasgow to pop down the M74 and lift the curse one Sunday, but this request has gone unanswered, presumably because he has got better things to do than partake in what is essentially witchcraft. My goodness, the world has gone nuts. Still, it makes interesting reading, and it's good to know that there are at least some people out there even dumber than us.

We rounded another big bend in the river

and crossed a bridge over the smaller River Caldew that feeds into the Eden. After this, we got our first look at Carlisle Castle, which stood imposing its presence on us from across the park. That the castle is so big also explains why Carlisle Cathedral is the second smallest in the country, as parts of that were torn down for the stone required to build this.

The castle was built way back by William II, who was the son of William the Conqueror. This was perhaps a bit cheeky, as at this time, Carlisle was still regarded as being a part of Scotland, but it clearly did not bother Bill Junior. Over the next few hundred years, the castle was improved until it eventually became what we have today.

The biggest test for the castle was the Jacobite uprising of 1745 when Bonnie Prince Charlie, of course, invaded England for the last time. He took Carlisle and the castle, and then his forces headed south, as far as Derbyshire believe it or not. Fearing a counter-attack by the British, however, he came back up north, and was pursued by Prince William, son of King George II. It all came to a head at the Battle of Culloden, which the English won, and after this, Charlie was forced to flee.

A huge bounty was put on his head, which at £30,000 was huge for the time, yet not a single highlander chose to cash him in, and in fact, many actively aided him along his journey. These people helped him to get to the small Isle of Benbecula, a beautiful island in the heart of the Outer

Hebrides, though the most famous part of his trip is perhaps his crossing to the Isle of Skye. On this crossing, Flora MacDonald is said to have rowed him across the water while he was disguised as her maid, Betty Burke. All of this is immortalized in the beautifully haunting *The Skye Boat Song* by Sir Harold Edwin Boulton, which you really should listen to at some point.

Charlie made it anyway, boarding a French warship in September 1746 on which he then fled back to Europe. He died of a stroke in 1788 and is buried at the Frascati Cathedral near Rome and the crypt of St Peter's Basilica in the Vatican. How can he be buried in two places; I hear you ask? Well, he was initially buried in the Cathedral, but in 1807 his remains were moved to the Basilica, though his heart was left behind in the Cathedral. I'm not sure about you, but to me, this sounds like a messy move and seems somewhat pointless.

Back to the castle itself though, as it is very interesting, and although we are not going in today, I have been before, and it's definitely worth a look. Many prisoners were held deep within its walls, and if you visit today, you will be able to see the licking stones, with the clue in the name. Prisoners would lick these stones in order to get enough moisture to keep them alive until that is, they were taken away to have their heads lopped off.

There is a military museum here too, and if you have ever heard these stories where soldiers were saved by a hip flask or a book in their pocket, well, this is the place to come. They have a bible here that still has the bullet from a machine gun lodged in it from the First World War. The bullet went all the way through the bible and just nipped through the back cover, which surely must have tickled at least a little. It belonged to Private Frederick Peil, who came from nearby Ireby in Cumbria, just a few miles south-west of here. Fred had been a butcher, but as was the case at the time, many men felt compelled to volunteer for King and Country, which is exactly what Fred did. He wasn't necessarily as lucky as his bible would suggest, though, as he spent two-thirds of his enlisted time in the hospital, and was discharged in 1918 due to a foot injury, although this is a damn sight better than a bullet to the heart.

We were in Bitts Park, which was the first-ever public park in Carlisle, and it has a rather nice statue of Queen Victoria within it. What she may not know, though, is that she is looking out over the site of the former town rubbish dump, over which the park was built in the 1890s.

After passing through this pleasant little park, which incidentally was surprisingly empty, we walked beneath Eden Bridge, which is, in fact, the only bridge that connects the bulk of Carlisle with the rest of it that sits on the north bank of the River Eden.

Stanwix is over there, which was at some point the location of one of the largest forts along the course of Hadrian's Wall, though all signs of it have long since vanished. It is near here that the wall crossed over the river, and headed directly northeast, though we will be taking a different course for a while, and will meet up with it just before the airport.

Although that part of Carlisle is now well and truly built over, occasional archaeological finds are still made every now and then. One of the most recent was in 2017, when the fort's bathhouse was discovered by the river and underneath the cricket field, which must have made a mess of the field, I would imagine. The preserved remains were quite extensive and included the under-floor heating that was typical of many high-end Roman buildings and turns out to be called a hypocaust. They also found an inscription to Julia Domna, whom I have never heard of, but she was married to Septimius Severus, which is a name that I do remember from those long boring history lessons at Sutton Park Primary School. I probably would have fallen asleep that day and missed learning all about Severus, but I was scared stiff of Mr Harrison, the history teacher, although he was actually quite a nice man, in retrospect.

Anyway, Severus rose to power after killing the previous emperor, Didius Julianus, probably because he had a bit of a stupid name. Severus was a formidable warrior and had come to Britannia with fighting in mind, and with his very large army, he was another one who tried to invade

Scotland but failed. Unfortunately, he became incredibly ill and died shortly after in York. This was the last Roman attempt to invade Scotland, and following his death, the frontier was permanently withdrawn back to the Wall. He was buried in the Mausoleum of Hadrian, an amazing building which still stands to this very day in Rome, though it is now known as the Castel Sant'Angelo. At some point, though, his remains were lost, which is a bit careless, to say the least. Perhaps his most famous legacy is the advice he is supposed to have given to his sons Caracalla and Geta on his deathbed, which was *Be harmonious, enrich the soldiers, scorn all others*. What he meant by this, was that in order to keep power, look after the army, and sod the Senate. Caracalla promptly gave the army a huge pay rise and did, in fact, remain in power right up until his death.

His death was a weird one, though. He had been on the warpath, as usual, and was on his way to Harran in Turkey to plan a bit of a battle, and had been wanting to go for a wee for quite some time. Presumably, after telling his driver that he was dying for a pee, if you pardon the pun, the procession stopped, and Caracalla promptly went to do his business. He was stabbed mid-flow and bled to death.

Anyway, back to the bridge. Although as previously stated, it is, perhaps criminally, the only road bridge linking both sides of the city, what the place lacks in quantity, it more than makes up for in quality, as it is a very fine bridge. It was designed by a guy called Robert Smirke, and to give you an idea of its pedigree, Smirke also designed the Covent Garden Theatre and the Royal Opera House, as well as Somerset House and the British Museum, so at least we can guess that it was built to last. Unfortunately, he never got round to coming to my home town of Hull, which is a real shame. Quite Bizarrely, Smirke is, however, responsible for the jail in the tiny city of St Johns, which is on the island of Newfoundland, Canada, although he couldn't ever get to Hull. Just saying.

After going under the bridge, we found ourselves at the sports centre, where we decided to stop for a rest and enjoy a refreshingly fruity slush drink. This was one of the points where we got our Hadrian's Wall passport stamped, and it was quite satisfying to knock another one of those empty spots off. There was a temporary exhibition on the wall, and I went over to have a look. A picture of Melvyn Bragg caught my eye, and it turns out that he was from these parts. I have long listened to some of Braggs podcasts, In Our Time, which are quite frankly very high-brow discussions of history, much of which goes above my head, but they are interesting nonetheless.

Bragg was born in Carlisle in 1939, and his dad was away for four years due to the war. After the war, he lived above a pub and lived a normal working-class existence, with his big break coming when he managed to get into a grammar school, which then paved the way for university. After this, hard work earned him a rare traineeship at the BBC. He was particularly famous for presenting the South Bank Show, although I never watched this, and he was also a prolific writer, apparently.

He got into politics and donated some considerable sums to the campaign that resulted in Tony Blair's landslide victory in 1997, for which he was awarded a peerage. His gifted lifestyle has not, however, meant that everything has been plain sailing. His first wife sadly committed suicide, which must be tremendously difficult to deal with and to reconcile, and he has indeed confirmed that he has suffered from mental health problems in his life, though he did this at a time before it became trendy. I had no idea that he was from Carlisle, but then I guess I wouldn't, would I? They were clearly very proud of him anyway.

Perhaps now would be a good time to look at the wider history of Carlisle. There is a lot more to it than just the curse and Melvyn Bragg, and it has many a fine tale to tell. The place has changed hands several times over the last few hundred years and has variously been both Scottish and English. It is the largest city in Cumbria, which isn't difficult as it is the only city in Cumbria, and it is another place that may have been home to King Arthur. There is at least one manuscript from the 15th century that says Arthur held his court here, and indeed it is believed that the king fought his last battle at Birdoswald Fort, which we will come to later. Possibly backing this up, King Arthur is said to be buried at nearby Arthuret Church, in Longtown, just north of Carlisle. Of course, many places claim links to King Arthur, though there is little proof for any of them; still, it would be nice, wouldn't it?

As has been mentioned, the cross-border raiders, or Reivers, were a bit of problem for quite some time, and this only ceased to be so when most of them were shipped off to Ireland, often complete families of them, which was probably a bit more effective than putting a curse on them if we are honest. As a result of this turbulent history, the place has more or less always been a military town, and in 1698, Celia Fiennes, the pioneering travel writer, wrote that the town was rife with alcohol and prostitutes, which maybe explains why she kept coming back.

As for people that came from here, a few others are worth mentioning, with Eddie Stobart probably being at the top of that list. Richard Hammond lives nearby, apparently, though wasn't born here, and at least one other person definitely deserves a mention.

Monkhouse Davison was born in the city in 1713. His dad was a successful grocer, and Monkhouse followed in the family business. They expanded into international markets and even sold tea overseas.

If you have heard of the Boston Tea Party, where Americans disguised themselves as native peoples and threw tea overboard in protest at high taxation, I bet you have never wondered who that tea belonged to? Well, I am going to answer the question that you have never asked, and the answer is Monkhouse Davison. To say he was a bit miffed at what happened to his tea is an understatement, and he even sought compensation from the King, George III, whom he ultimately blamed for his financial loss. Whether or not the King paid up is unclear, as he presumably had bigger fish to fry, as of course the tea-throwing incident indirectly but ultimately led to the American War of Independence, and the loss of the colonies. If that question ever comes up in a quiz, and you win it big-time, please remember me.

It was a different type of drink that has caused problems in Carlisle more recently, however. At the start of the First World War, the government wanted workers to be as efficient as possible, so they conducted an intriguing experiment in the city. The reason was that there were lots of munitions factories around here, and they particularly figured that alcohol and explosives don't mix very well. All pubs were brought into public ownership, which meant that from then on, they were effectively run by the government. I don't know about you, but if someone asked me to think of the worst idea possible, ever, then it would probably be for the government to run my local pub. I literally cannot imagine anything worse. Anyway, the idea was to curb excessive drinking, which would, in turn, improve both the efficiency and output of the workers. Partitions and secluded snugs inside pubs disappeared, and a generally more open-plan approach was adopted. The exterior of the pub was changed too, and only a hint of the function of the building was allowed.

Emphasis was placed less on alcohol itself, and much more on things such as tables where people could sit and chat together, as well as the promotion of pub games and meals rather than drinks. This came to be the blueprint for all pubs nationwide after the war, and if you think about it, this description might well apply to a pub that you visit nowadays. Amazingly, and this really is the amazing bit, these measures, which were supposed to be a temporary wartime experiment, continued for decades, and the government remained in charge of all Carlisle pubs right up until 1973.

As always with us awkward Brits, though, there was at least one person who refused to give his pub up to the government, and good on him for doing so. The manager of the White Quey in Durbar, just near the racecourse in the south of the city, chose instead to shut his pub for good, and even stated in his will that the building should never again be used as such an establishment while the government are in control. Following the end of the scheme though, his descendants changed their minds, and the pub reopened in June 1976, finally free of government restrictions.

We moved on soon enough and wandered alongside yet more sports fields, and after a couple of bends in the river, we came to a footbridge where we were going to cross to the northern bank of the river. This bridge, called Spenny Bridge, as in suspension bridge, is perhaps the most unusual war memorial I have ever seen, with a plaque high up on its girders saying it is dedicated to those who gave their lives in the Great War of 1914-1918.

We walked straight through the park and saw another war memorial, the Cenotaph, which was also quite impressive before we turned right along a very neat tarmac path which led us past Rickerby Hall, which is now some kind of spa retreat, which quite frankly we could do well to stop at.

Rickerby Park used to belong to the hall, but the estate has long since been broken up. The last time it was all together, so to speak, was under the stewardship of George Head Head, and no, that is not a typo, he really was called that. George was the son of a wealthy bank and mine owner and was, therefore, filthy rich, but rather than sitting on his laurels and doing nothing, he became actively involved in the anti-slavery campaign. His family life, though, was not quite what he wanted. His first wife died young, and he failed to have a child with his second wife so instead adopted a distant relative called Miles MacInnes. When Head Head died, he left his considerable fortune to MacInnes on the condition that the youngster adopted Head Head's name and coat of arms. Mac-Innes gleefully accepted all the cash, but never did change his name to Head Head, but then would you have?

Passing the hall, unfortunately without having had a nice pedicure, we passed an interesting old house with what looked like a totem pole in the garden, and on our left, in the fields, there is a rather large and old tower. It is not as old as it looks, however, and is actually something else that George Head Head left behind. I am sorry, but I just can't stop writing his name. Anyway, whether he was trying to recreate one of the many Peel towers that dot this area is not known, but it looks good, nonetheless.

The path here was separated from the road, which was a good thing as it was very narrow and full of farm vehicles today. As we went further east, we began to hear the sound of traffic, and after a little while, we could see the fast-moving cars and trucks on the motorway, just beyond which was Linstock, and the end of our walking for today. Rob phoned the café in Bowness to place our orders, steaks all round, as we expected we only had around another 30 minutes of walking to go unless of course, he had missed a page out.

We crossed over the motorway and headed down into the village, where we found the van exactly where we had left it, and after a quick change of footwear into something more comfortable, we were off back towards Bowness to see whether or not Anthony's car had washed away. I volunteered to roll around in the back of the van on this first journey, just to get it out of the way really, as I reckoned it was perhaps one of the shorter journeys and was on relatively flat roads, so there was method in my madness.

Despite the rush hour traffic around Carlisle, it didn't take too long to get back to the start, where we found that the tide had not come in too far that day, after all, so we parked the van next to the car. Wandering slowly on our throbbing feet through the village back to the café, the place was as quiet as ever, and when we took our seats and waited for our steaks, we were the only customers.

The food was good and went down all too quickly, and before long, we were heading back to the campsite with sore feet and full bellies. The hot showers were a welcome relief, as was the feeling of clean clothes, and in no time at all, we were all sat outside of our little tent enjoying a nice beer and watching the sun dip below the horizon. As first days go, today could not have been better.

CHAPTER 3
Linstock to Birdoswald

The plan for today was to resume our walk at Linstock, and head more or less due east, finishing at Birdoswald, one of the better-known Roman forts along the route and the only place where we can see the ruins of a fort along with the longest continuous stretch of wall, as well as a milecastle and a turret, all together. Initially bouncing along the River Eden once again, we would pass through the intriguingly named Park Broom and along an old Roman road, Stanegate, to the village of Crosby-on-Eden. Heading north just a little bit, we would join the actual course of Hadrian's Wall, which we would then more or less follow for the rest of the day. This would take us past Bleatarn and Carlisle Airport, on to Newtown and Walton and through the small village of Banks which would see us finally finishing at Birdoswald. We would therefore be hoping to see a bit more of the wall today, rather than just the earthworks that we saw at various points along the way yesterday.

The day had started drearily, with slow but steady rain falling as we prepared our food and tidied up after us. This continued in the car towards Birdoswald, where we left the van, and then back to Linstock where we started walking.

Resuming our route, the rain was on and off, but when we joined the path along the River Eden just past Park Broom, the sky suddenly got a whole lot brighter. I took my jacket off and tied it around my waist, as I suspected I would probably need to put it back on again soon, but left my gaiters on for now as the ground was very wet and we were alternately walking through high grass and crops.

Signs once again pointed us in the right direction every now and then, but again they weren't strictly necessary, as it was a straight route. At Low Crosby, we left the River Eden for good, as we continued east and the river turned south. We had walked along this river before, although much further south when on the Coast to Coast walk, and had last passed it at Kirkby Stephen, where it is supposed to be haunted by the ghost of Jangling Annas, and we got chatting about the high points of that walk, which we had enjoyed very much. Anthony had not come along on that one, though, as we did not know him at the time, so we jokingly vowed to do it again one day, though I think we were only half-joking. Well, I certainly was anyway, and that is definitely one walk that I could certainly see myself doing again one day, although

I am not generally a fan of walking any given route more than once, unless it is to a pub, of course.

Going into the village, we found ourselves passing through a housing estate, which was a novelty, and which brought us to the main road, where we turned right and which was actually Stanegate, or a road which ran along the same course of it at least.

Stanegate was one of many Roman roads that dotted the country, but this one was more important than most. It predated Hadrian's Wall and ran between what is modern-day Carlisle and Corbridge, an impressive distance of nearly 40 miles. We only followed it for a very short distance though, before heading north towards the all-important route of Hadrian's wall itself, where we were all looking forward to seeing some of it that had not been upcycled into a church or a Peel Tower.

Crossing the main road, we finally found ourselves heading east along the actual course of the wall, but the only ruins we saw were of a collapsing barn, and that was made of normal bricks and was in no way Roman. This main road, incidentally, had originally been part of General Wade's Military Road when it was first built. There are two things we should clarify, though, which are critically important. The first one is that General Wade was actually a Field Marshall, and the second is that he died in 1748. Being that the survey for this road was only done in 1749, and construction began in in 1751, how this road became known as General Wade's, is something of a mystery. In a manner reminiscent of how Emperor Hadrian never saw his wall, therefore, General Wade also never saw his road.

The name probably came from the fact that Wade had earlier voiced concerns about the lack of a road between Newcastle and Carlisle, and this had been particularly highlighted as being a bit of a problem when, as we have already heard, in 1745, Bonnie Prince Charlie marched into England via Carlisle relatively unopposed, and was able to capture the castle, at least for a while. Wade was stuck in Newcastle, and with no quick or obvious way to get his army swiftly across the country, he was somewhat helpless.

Anyway, everyone quickly realized the strategic importance of having such a road here, which is why it was eventually built. Although the road is a fair distance from the wall at this point, this isn't always the case, but more of that later.

We were, however, following the course of the Roman Military Way, which is the name given to the road which runs immediately south of and parallel to, Hadrian's Wall. Other than the straightness of the route, however, there was absolutely no sign of anything remotely Roman.

The road gave way to a track, which then deteriorated into a path, yet it remained as straight as anything. There were signs of the vallum every now and then, with rows of old-growth trees atop a mound, which was at least something. Other than that, we just wandered through field after field of admittedly beautiful countryside with not a care in the world. The silence out here was immense, and I was enjoying every moment of the day so far.

We passed Carlisle Airport, which did not look to be the busiest airport in the world, though it did have a good museum. I had been a couple of years earlier when I had stayed at the nearby Center Parcs and had looked for something to do one day that would be cheap and cheerful, as opposed to staying on the park all day, where my children would spend a small fortune given the chance. We had ended up at the Solway Aviation Museum mainly for one reason, and one reason only, they had a Vulcan Bomber.

There was a bit of a queue to get the chance to sit in the cockpit, and after pushing my kids out of the way and down the steps, I was next in line. To say it was a tight squeeze would be an understatement, and I can't imagine spending hours on end in there, as pilots would have done when flying it.

Built as a strategic nuclear bomber, we should all perhaps be grateful that it was never used in anger, well, not in the intended manner anyway. The Vulcans did see action, during the 1982 Falklands Conflict, when they were stationed at Ascension Island in the middle of the Atlantic Ocean. Although they did not have the range to fly to and from the Falklands Islands from their temporary base, an intricate series of air-to-air refuelling missions enabled them to carry out the so-called Black Buck raids on Port Stanley Airfield. This specific aircraft was long rumoured to have taken part in those missions, particularly as there are four faded but very mysterious stars painted near the cockpit. However, it was recently discovered that this one did not take part after all, and spent the war at RAF Scampton being refitted and possibly scavenged for parts at some point.

There is also a rather large rocket engine here, which is taken from a Blue Streak Rocket, and the museum tells the story of nearby RAF Spadeadam, but more of that later, as we have a walk to do, remember?

Newtown took us by surprise, but it was more a village than a town. There were definitely a couple of older cottages here that were suspiciously well built, with Croft House looking particularly sturdy, which made me suspect its bricks were very ancient if you know what I mean.

At the end of the village, we crossed the main road and went through what looked like somebody's garden, where we found ourselves back out into the open countryside with only sheep as company. We could see for miles, and the weather had certainly taken a turn for the better, which meant it was time to take off the gaiters.

Had we gone south on the main road, we

could have gone to Brampton, just beyond which lies Gelt Woods. Although it is a little off the beaten path, it is worth the visit, as this is where you will find a quarry where some of the stones used to build and repair the wall were sourced. There is a series of herring-bone like patterns cut into the cliff face of the quarry, showing where the chisels hit the rock, which leaves the quarry with a sort of temple-like finish. It is not this that is worth the visit, however, it is the graffiti. It would appear that even Roman stone-masons got a bit bored every now and then, which is why if you do come here, you will see a rather large penis cut incredibly clearly into the cliff-face, which definitely makes the visit worthwhile, in my book anyway. If you think about it, this information is not something you are going to find in a proper guidebook, so with that in mind, you are most welcome. There are other carvings here too, with one rather interesting caricature of a commanding officer as well as an inscription dating to 207 AD, which was at the height of a repair programme on the wall, suggesting that the rocks from here probably were used for that very purpose.

It turns out that men, because let's face it, it was probably men, have been drawing penises since the dawn of time, although the Romans also used them as a symbol for good luck. They were, however, often used to intimidate the natives as well, and indeed rape was an accepted way for the Roman military to enforce their authority, although this did backfire seriously with the case of Boudicca, as we have already heard, something that nearly reversed the Roman conquest of Britain. The earliest known representation of male sexuality, though, is thought to be an incredible 28,000 years old. The Hohle phallus, as it is known, was found in a cave in Germany, and there is even a school of thought that it is, in fact, a stone-age sex toy, carved from solid rock. One of those responsible for its discovery, Professor Nicholas Conard, even described it as highly polished, whatever that means.

It turns out that rude graffiti is quite common along the wall, too, and Newcastle University lecturer Rob Collins claims to have catalogued 57 other such examples along the course of the wall. Unfortunately, he does not yet seem to have made this information open to the public, but I will be sure to keep my eyes peeled as we move along.

Carrying on once again, we almost went through Beck Farm, though luckily at the last minute we saw the multitude of keep out signs and barriers that had been prominently placed all around. Crossing over a small but pleasant footbridge, the next farm allowed unfettered access straight through, after which we crossed yet another footbridge, this one over Cam Beck, and it was even more idyllic than the last. It would seem that today is the gift that just keeps on giving.

Next up was Sandysike Bunkhouse, but

strangely the path went all the way around the place rather than through it, which I thought not the greatest idea when you are probably trying to get people to stay there while doing this walk. Still, we carried on, with not a hint or a sniff of the wall to be found anywhere, nonetheless all the while enjoying ourselves immensely. We passed sturdy-looking walls and went through pleasant meadows and little woods, and just before Walton, we bumped into a group of lads doing the walk east to west, with full camping gear. Their rucksacks were huge, and they had pots and pans and kettles dangling from them, which clanked almost in rhythm as they wobbled along.

We chatted to them for a while, and they told us there were seven of them doing the walk, with the other three ahead of them somewhere, which was odd as we had not seen anyone. They had started in Newcastle 6 days ago and were hoping to finish tomorrow and asked us if we had come across any good camping spots along the way, as they were wild camping. The best place we had seen was probably along the River Eden, just to the west of Carlisle, which we told them, advising them to make use of the bathrooms at the sports centre in the city. This stretch of the river was heavily wooded with lots of room along the riverbank, in addition to the many empty fields along the way, so we figured they would not have a problem finding somewhere in that vicinity. They might even be able to camp on the old railway bridge, we added, which would certainly make for a most interesting and quite unusual campsite.

Walton was another tiny village, but it did at least have a pub, which was fittingly called *The Centurion*. Unfortunately, it was closed, so we carried on, with the road leading us slowly into a shallow valley. At the foot of the valley, a small humpback bridge took us over a tiny stream, after which we gratefully turned off the road and edged along a field towards a small wood. Incidentally, just before the bridge on the north side of the wall, there is a long mound in the field, which you may not notice unless you bother to look for it. This is actually the wall, and this particular section is one of those that has been buried in order to preserve it, presumably from the hundreds of sheep that were busy going to the toilet in there when I passed. The wood itself, however, turned out not to be a wood at all and was really just a thin hedge of trees along the stream, and after a while, we found ourselves once again heading east along the route of the actual though still invisible wall.

When the wall was built, those responsible often signed their work. This was not because, when almost 2,000 years later, should a chubby, old and not very fresh hiker come along, they would know who built this wall, but it was more for purposes of quality control. There is one such marker just a couple of minutes walk off the main track here, at Howgill Farm. Now part of a barn, the stone reads *civitate catuvellaun orum Toss dio*, which translates to *From the tribe of the Catuvellauni Tossodio,* thereby naming the builders. If you read any Latin, you might not have needed the translation, for which I apologize, but you may have, as the type of Latin that the Romans spoke, vulgar Latin, is quite different from the classical Latin that posh kids learn nowadays. By the way, it isn't called vulgar Latin because it's horrible, it just means it is common, a bit like your humble author.

While at the barn, I notice someone has placed a piece of slate at the top of the stone in an effort to preserve it, but I still can't help but wonder how long it will last out here. It might be nice and pleasant today, I think to myself, but then I imagine what it must be like up here in the middle of February. I reckon that if a discovery such as this stone was made in, say, America, it would be protected and probably placed in a museum, but out here, it is just left to the weather, more or less, probably because there are thousands of stones just like it.

I'm glad it was just letters on that stone though, as I have always had a problem with Roman numerals, and struggle to remember which letter represents each number. In a nutshell, I could, in fact, say, Roman numerals, eh? What are they good IV?

For the next half-mile or so, the path was much better than my jokes, but we did feel very hemmed in between a fence and a hedge, though thankfully this did not take long to pass. Here again, the only sign of the wall was the line of trees, with a barely discernible bank in places. Once again, though, the beautiful rolling country-side and fantastic views made up for the total lack of a wall.

After crossing another minor road, and a further hike, we came to a farm track and decided to have a quick diversion to Lanercost, which was only a few hundred yards away, where there was the impressive ruin that was Lanercost Priory. It only took a few minutes to walk along the lane that led us down the hill into the village, where one of those old fashioned black and white road signs surprisingly said it was only 9 miles to New-castle, but after rubbing my eyes and looking again, it actually said Bewcastle.

The priory was just over a fence and looked quite impressive, so we ventured south just a few yards and went through the drive gates and under a rather ramshackle arch. To go into the priory itself there was an admission fee, so we just wan-dered around the grounds, which still gave us a very good look at the ruins it has to be said. For the short walk that it is to get here, I reckon this place is an absolutely essential stopping point along this walk and had we planned better, we probably would have paid to go in, as it is steeped in history.

Lanercost had been historically well and truly in the thick of it due to its unfortunate loca-tion close to the Scottish border. It was regularly subjected to raids by the Scots, with the first one in 1296. The second came just a year later and was led by none other than William Wallace himself. Robert the Bruce had a go in 1311, and the final raid was in 1346. During this turbulent time, the entire place was pillaged twice and burned down twice, so it is quite surprising there is anything left, quite frankly.

Edward I had also visited the place on his ill-fated journey north to fight the Scottish. Now aptly called King Edwards Tower, his accommodation today forms part of the vicarage and is where he stayed while suffering from dysentery. The intention was for a short stay, but the King's condition deteriorated quickly, and it soon became apparent that he would not be moving on any time soon. It is thought that he was here for quite some time, possibly around 5 months, and he almost bankrupted the priory in the process.

He rode up on 29th September 1306, along with a dodgy tummy and a sizeable entourage. This included the queen as well as other members of the royal family, along with many officials. For instance, he had with him a guy called John de Drokensford, who was the keeper of the royal wardrobe, as well as his chaplain, his surgeons, some porters, and just for good measure, some trumpeters. Never again will I complain about what my wife takes on holiday.

Meticulous records were kept which tell us all this, and there is even a record of a man called

Robert de Royston being sent to my home city of Kingston-on-Hull to buy wax for the king's privy seal. Hull did the finest wax in those days, you see, something to do with medieval ears.

Much money was spent on medicines, with one bill being for over £164, an absolute fortune back then, and which also included in the order chemicals generally used for embalming a body after death, although I'll bet they never told the king about that.

There was also an inventory made of the items that the royal party carried, and included in that list were some quite strange items. Top of this list was a thorn from Christ's crown of thorns, along with a small bone from the head of St Lawrence, an arm, yes, I said an arm, of St David, another arm – well, what use is one by itself? Surely you need a pair? - from St Richard of Chichester, and a silver-gilt vessel in the shape of a small boat containing some bones of the 11,000 virgins. Quite an eclectic mix, then, although I wonder about the thinking that went into packing every time he travelled. I imagine the queen shouting from the bathroom *don't forget St David's arm and have you packed your virgin bones?*

It wasn't all sitting around being ill and doing nothing at Lanercost though, and the king certainly kept himself busy. He received a couple of parcels while here, including the severed heads of the Lord of Kintyre along with another from an Irish nobleman, although we must remember that there was a war on, so this was all perfectly fine. A man called Thomas de Bruce was captured and brought here to the king, while still attached to his head apparently, although he was soon sentenced to death. Specifically, he was to be drawn at the tails of horses through Carlisle on the Friday after the first Sunday in Lent, and afterwards to be hanged and then, and only then, beheaded, which I think we can all agree was both very specific and would certainly do the job.

Edward did, however, at least partly recognize the burden that he put upon the priory, and did make some attempts to lighten this somewhat, though his efforts never went far enough, and the place remained very poor after he left. Although this was certainly one of the more colourful periods in the Priory's history, it certainly didn't do it any good, and when the dissolution of the monasteries came in 1536, being relatively poor, Lanercost was one of the first to go.

Back to the monastery itself though. It was partly built from something called spolia, which is recycled stone, from guess where, that's right, the wall that you can no longer see around here. I'm told that if you look carefully at the stonework of the building, it is still possible to see a few Roman inscriptions in the brickwork. I never saw any, but then I didn't exactly go around having what you would call a proper look, to be honest. There was a cemetery here too, and I always like to poke my nose in these wherever we go, as you never know what you will find.

We hit the jackpot in here, though, sort of, for this is the final resting place of Thomas Addison. Addison is credited with being the first to identify a disease which results in the progressive destruction of the adrenal glands, which obviously became known as Addison's disease. I'm not sure about you, but I will be happy if I finally go to my grave without having one or another major illness named after me, but there you go. Sadly, Addison committed suicide following a period of prolonged depression. He jumped over a wall and landed on his head, and that was that. He had been walking in the garden with some other people described as his attendants, and presumably surprised them when he suddenly flung himself to his vertical death. He had tried to kill himself before, so we can only presume that his attendants were there to stop him trying again, and I think it is also only fair to presume that they were fired afterwards. Anyway, Addison is buried forevermore in the rather impressive sarcophagus under the great yew tree. You can't miss it.

We sat on a little rustic bench just outside of the graveyard for a while but knew that we should really get a move on, so soon headed back up the small lane that took us to our path, where we resumed our journey east. Walking along the road next to the priory though, it is just possible to see the boundary wall for the place, and if you have a proper look, you will see that it is particularly well built and solid, and is another excellent example of monks having robbed Hadrian's Wall for their own ends. On a final note concerning Lanercost, Edward I stopped here one final time when he was on his way back down to Westminster Abbey. He wouldn't have been able to admire the recycled wall then, though, as he was of course now dead.

Back on the path, after a long period following the trees, we finally got one heck of a treat when we not only managed to spot a bit of the wall that was still in situ, but we spotted the tallest bit of the wall known to exist, which is when we arrived at Hare Hill. How this bit survived being pilfered was a mystery to me when all around it was gone, and though it was probably rebuilt at some point, the core of it remains original. I later found out that this piece is also the most westerly section of the wall that survives, which explains our lack of sightings so far, so make sure you find this place if you ever decide to do the walk. There is an information panel here that says the builders of this section inscribed a stone on the north side with PP, to signify the builder Primus Pilus, but I looked and looked and could not see it. I later found out it is at eye level and is quite badly worn, but this was a couple of days later, and there was no way I was going back to check, so you will have to let me know.

This seemed a natural place to take another little break, which is exactly what we did, and enjoyed our snacks and drinks for a few minutes before we decided to move on, buoyed by our first sighting of the wall, which I have got to admit, got us a bit too excited than I care to admit, especially considering that we are all allegedly adults of course. Perhaps it was the big kid coming out in us, but all I can say is, it is what it is.

We were back on roads now, at least for a while, but they were gratefully devoid of any major traffic. The village of Banks proved to be another none event, although it was very nice in its way, and the villagers had clearly made full use of a UNESCO World Heritage Site when building their walls, garages and barns.

Near to the phone box, a German couple had parked their camper van and were busy brewing up a cup of coffee, so we stopped to chat for a minute. They were driving around looking for a property to buy, they said, as they were looking to relocate to somewhere more beautiful than their home town of Ludwigshafen, which they informed us was voted Germany's ugliest city a while back, a statement they seemed strangely proud of. They went on to add that the tourist authorities in Ludwigshafen produced a leaflet a couple of years back that listed the top five things to do while in the city, and all involved going somewhere else. I figured then that their mission would not be too difficult, as if it was as bad as they said, then almost anywhere would do, but they had certainly chosen one of the better options by coming up here, for sure.

We left them behind and carried on to the top of a hill, where we were pleasantly surprised by the beautiful view that awaited us up there. We were looking east down a deep, wide valley, with a patchwork of fields that was perhaps the nicest vista we had seen so far. Just to top that off, and when we thought things could not get any better, we came across some more wall. Although it was not as high as Hare Hill, it was just as substantial and was, in fact, the remains of a turret, this one being numbered 52A apparently, although this numbering system is a modern invention. From here on, all turrets and forts are numbered, with the numbers decreasing as we get towards Newcastle, so there is clearly going to be a lot to see before we get to number one.

We carried on along the narrow road, stepping aside as cars came along, and before long we were rewarded with another sighting of yet more ruins, and then another after a few hundred yards more. This was getting good, and was almost worth it, I thought to myself.

A short while later, one of those little wooden signs with an acorn directed us down a farm track and through a wooded area, where we were delighted to find an honesty box. This was Matthew's honesty box, and we were very happy to buy a sugar infusion for the bargain price of one pound.

After passing through a small wood, we

were now heading east parallel with though some distance from the road and following the course of the vallum, which was now clearly visible as an earthwork. It made a pleasant change from being on the road, and this continued for a mile or two, after which we remained in the field for a while but then found ourselves directly next to the road.

Passing the remains of another turret, we were surprised to find that we were almost at Birdoswald, which was visible in the distance just ahead, which of course meant our walking today was nearly finished.

As we neared the fort, we encountered a few more people, but when we turned into the courtyard, the place was positively buzzing, and I thought to myself that this was the most people we had seen in one place since setting off. We took advantage of the facilities, got that crucial stamp in our little passports, and then went to have a quick look around, but only a quick look, and from a distance. The section of wall here is supposed to be the longest remaining piece of Hadrian's Wall and the fort itself offers the most impressive remains of any of those along the wall. However, it has to be said that this is a claim made by English Heritage which now owns the place. The National Trust would argue that it is actually their fort up at Housesteads that is the best, so I shall reserve judgement and get back to you a bit later on if you don't mind. If you do mind, tough.

Anyway, after having a quick look around, we found the car park down the hill. We took great pleasure in taking our walking shoes off and getting into something a bit comfier, although there was a definite and strange aroma around, though we couldn't quite figure out what it was.

The drive to get the car was bumpy though uneventful. However, we could hear Robin swear every now and then as the van went over a particularly bumpy bump. Before long, we were at the Co-op supermarket in Haltwhistle choosing something tasty for dinner, which we were cooking ourselves tonight, on account of being financially challenged.

Back at the campsite, I once again found the world's oldest cat when I went to have my shower, which apparently had now not moved for two days. We sat out again, watching the skies darken. Just when we thought nothing exciting could happen, a bunch of scouts turned up, loads of them. They entertained us for the next hour, putting their teepees up with what I can only describe as a varying proficiency. Finally, when it was too dark to see them tripping over guy lines and getting tangled up in them, we retired to bed, just as it started to rain.

CHAPTER 4

Birdoswald to Middle of Nowhere

I kid you not, we were walking today to the literal middle of nowhere. I could tell you that we had parked the car near The Old Repeater Station, but I bet you don't know where that is, so I won't. How about saying that it is a few miles north of Haydon Bridge? Not helpful? Milecastle 34? I give up.

Anyway, we are walking from Birdoswald, to, erm, where we parked the car. It might be helpful to say that our destination is a few miles past Housesteads Fort, so at least we might find out who really has the best fort by the end of the day. We will first walk through Gilsland where we will cross the railway line, then pass just north of Greenhead, where we will cross that very same rail line once again, and all the while we will be more or less exactly on the course of the wall, with some excellent stretches of the military way thrown in for good measure. Sycamore Gap is on the route, which will be a highlight for me at least, and we will also go past but not through Vindolanda, another one of the better-known forts. There will be more ups and downs today, and considerably more wall, which means it should be a very good day indeed, so long as no one gets lost or dies or goes insane, which are not as unlikely as they may sound when out walking with us lot. We will cross paths, literally, with the Pennine Way, so we might even get to meet some proper hikers, and anything else we come across will probably be a surprise because we haven't exactly planned today's walk all that thoroughly, you see.

For instance, we originally tried to leave the car in the car park of Housesteads Fort, but you had to pay, so we didn't bother. What we didn't know at the time, though, was that the car park had number plate recognition cameras, but it didn't really matter as it was Anthony's car. This is why we last saw it hugging a dry-stone wall in the middle of nowhere just so we could save £3.50, but there you go.

Anyway, we exit the van back at Birdoswald, where I have forgotten my English Heritage parking permit, so instead, I leave my membership card in the front window. If it gets a parking ticket, well, this isn't my van either.

Birdoswald is deserted at this time of the morning compared to when we were here last night, but the facilities are open, so we take full advantage before we move on. As we head east, a young family are taking pictures of their little kids who are stood on top of the wall with beaming smiles, and they are clearly having a wonderful time, or at least they were. A dog walker starts berating them for standing on the wall, but in all honesty, I don't think four-year-olds are the greatest threat to this giant stone structure that has stood here for two millennia. Bizarrely, the old man then stands watching his goofy little dog have a pee up the wall and does nothing to stop it, which kind of leaves me speechless. I do not get involved, however, as my wife always tells me off when I do, so I walk on, although I do exchange glances with the dad, who seems as bemused with the old man as I am.

It is worth mentioning Spadeadam Forest at this point, which is just a couple of miles north of here. As well as being a beautiful forest worthy of a visit in itself, this is also the location of a relic of British military history. During the cold war, the British partnered with the Americans to build intercontinental ballistic missiles to counter the Russian threat. By sharing technology, the Americans managed to build the Atlas rocket, which eventually put John Glenn into orbit, and we got Blue Streak, which didn't put anyone into orbit, but which if you remember, is the bit of rocket that can now be found in the museum at Carlisle Airport.

The British missiles were going to be test-fired from Australia, but before they were sent out there, they needed a full system test, and this is where Spadeadam comes in. In the middle of

Spadeadam Forest are two gigantic launch pads, identical copies of their Australian cousins, and scattered around the site are old Soviet and Eastern Bloc aircraft, just sat there rotting away. This place is definitely worth a visit, and I stumbled across it completely by accident one year when I got rather lost in Kielder Forest. Perhaps as a nod to the supposed secrecy of the place, on the road up to Spadeadam from Gilsland, there is a small farm called Moscow, and thinking about it, I'm not so sure that the public is even allowed in there, so don't go on my say so.

Moving on, the path takes us along a good selection of wall, forts and turrets, or what is left of them anyway, and at this point of the walk, they seem almost continuous. A path takes us down a steep hill and through some long grass, which makes me glad I have my trousers on at this early hour as I don't want to get bitten by anything nasty that might be schnaffling around for a bit of breakfast.

This section of the wall is going to be particularly interesting, as this is one of the places where there are some potentially rude and rather clear carvings to be found on the stonework. They are all marked by small metal strips that have been mortared into the wall, and I soon see my first example, which is very clearly a willy. I keep my eyes peeled, and before long I see another, which is even clearer, and which looks like many a doodle I saw when I was at school. Some things never change, with me giggling at pictures of willies being one of them. Honestly, these are definitely worth keeping an eye out for. If you are really stuck, then you need to be looking at distances of 374 metres and 40 metres west of Milecastle 49, and that distance is measured from the western wall. You will need a long tape measure, obviously, but it will be worth your while. I know, I know, I'm just a big kid.

We cross the River Irthing over a small footbridge, shortly after which we come to the old footings of the Roman bridge that used to stand here, which is called Willowford Bridge but should maybe be called Willyford Bridge, as this is another location where you can get the chance to see yet another phallic symbol carved into the stonework if you look carefully enough. The bridge is not anywhere near the river today though, and this is because, over the last two thousand years, the course of the river has adjusted ever so slowly and moved quite a few feet to its current position further west.

Indeed, it is here at the River Irthing, if you remember from the beginning, that archaeologists managed to figure out that the width of the wall was reduced from 10 to 8 feet, which also gave them the direction of the build, as the footing remained at the wider width. The bridge was also washed away quite early on, and rather than being rebuilt in stone, it was built with wood instead, and much, much later, parts of the bridge were used to build a farm. As for that elusive willy, if you look down on the abutment from the side where the riverbank is, and move towards the northern or upstream end, take a look at the lowest courses of the brickwork. It is on the second row up and is hard to miss once you know it's there. It is there for good luck, of course, but perhaps they should have drawn a bigger one, then maybe the bridge wouldn't have fallen down.

We next pass a farm, which is the one partly built from the remnants of the bridge, and join a track hemmed in between the substantial remains of the wall and a wooden fence. It is a bit narrow at this point, and we keep stopping to let other people pass who are coming from the other direction. They are mainly dog walkers, but then we meet a couple of girls who pass carrying backpacks which are bigger than them, and we figure they are doing the full walk east to west. My attempt to start a conversation falls flat when it becomes clear they speak little English, and I think to myself that it doesn't matter what their native language is, because like the vast majority of the English-speaking peoples, my lingual skills are almost non-existent. Still, we enjoy a moment or two of smiles and hand gestures, although whatever they were trying to say was completely lost on me.

Moving on, it is fair to say that this is definitely the longest section of wall we have encountered so far, and in parts it is quite tall too, even as tall as Rob in some places. Eventually, though, we come to Gilsland and a road and decide to walk through the village rather than follow the path as such. In the village centre, we find a small café where we grab a cup of coffee to take away and rounding a bend we find a huge sign just past the Bridge Inn welcoming us into Northumberland, meaning of course that we just left Cumbria, and I wonder if that means we are halfway.

A right turn at the bus stop points us back in the direction of the official path, where we stop momentarily to open a bag of Haribos, as we reckon we are going to need the sugar today, and this is where Robin manages to find a public toilet, as is his uncanny knack. While he is gone, for quite some time it has to be said, whatever was he doing in there, Anthony finds a woggle left behind by a scout, apparently. I didn't know what a woggle was, I was a bad boy you see, and Chris had to explain it to me. It's that cloth thing they put around their necks, and which Anthony then put around his neck, and by the looks of it, he was never a scout either. So, when Robin finally returned, he was surprised to see that Anthony had enlisted, so to speak, at which point we carried on.

Almost immediately, we came across a children's' playground, where we had absolutely no choice but to stop. The reason, you see, is that this playground must have been the Guinness world record holder for the longest slide. This thing was huge, and very, very high, quite probably dangerously so. Whichever local authority health and safety officer that authorized this thing must have been high on crack or something because this bad boy was wild.

Without any hesitation whatsoever, Chris dropped his rucksack and map on the floor and ran up the steps. Stepping onto the slide, he seated himself correctly, then, nothing. He just sat there, apparently unable to move.

After a second, though, there was a hint of movement as gravity slowly took over, although it was almost imperceptible at first. Slowly, ever so slowly, he gained speed, until he must have reached some kind of crux point where he just accelerated down like a bullet. We figured this part of the slide must have been wet, and that is what assisted with his now dangerous velocity, and as he got faster, he seemed to lose his balance a bit. By the time he got to the bottom of the slide, and just as Robin and Anthony jumped out of the way, he was almost on his side and going very fast, and as he shot off the end and into the sand, some fine words were coming out of his mouth that it would be rude to repeat.

We all fell about laughing, and as Chris got up off the floor, he was indeed soaking wet, or at least his shorts and back were, but he was also covered in sand which was now stuck to him all over. This was possibly not his finest decision this week, but it gave us all a good laugh and woke us up, I can tell you.

Leaving Gilsland behind, a tunnel took us under the railway line, and after we crossed a road, we found ourselves once again walking along the course of the wall, with the earthworks being the obvious giveaway at this point. I had read that some parts of the wall had been buried to protect it, and this may well have been one of those parts, so prominent was the bank here.

We passed a farm and continued eastwards, and saw a golf club to our south, though there were not many people out today. Crossing a road, we joined a path that was now also the route of the Pennine Way, and almost immediately bumped into some proper hikers, who would be sharing this route for the next few miles almost to House-steads Fort, where they would turn north, and we would continue east. A quick hello was exchanged, but it seemed that they didn't want to talk, and they were soon ahead of us, so were clearly on a mission. I did not envy them. They had a much longer distance to go, with extra-large backpacks, and although I would love to do the Pennine Way one day, today was not that day.

We crossed the railway lines again; they looped around to the north and then came back towards the south again, and we then found ourselves at the small River Tipalt, and above it and on a hill, the small but impressive remains of Thirlwall Castle were clearly visible. We wandered up to have a look, talking to a young couple who asked us to take their picture and enjoyed the views from the top.

The only link that Thirlwall Castle has with the wall is its name. Well, that and the several thousand bricks that the Thirlwall family stole from the wall in order to build the castle that is, as even a modest castle of this size was otherwise well beyond their means.

There are a couple of interesting stories related to the castle which I shall tell you now. The first one is about Percival Thirlwall, who was killed at the Battle of Bosworth Field, which was, of course, the penultimate battle of the Wars of the Roses. Old Percy was Richard III's standard-bearer, so he basically carried a flag. As luck would have it, he was killed in the final charge of this battle, which is pretty bad luck when you think about it, and the story goes that he still held up his flag even after having his legs cut off. This reminds me of the scene from Monty Python and the Holy Grail, where the Black Knight loses first his arms and then his legs, and says it's just a flesh wound.

There is another story about this place, though, that is much more relevant to our walk. If you remember at the beginning of our walk how Edward I died of dysentery up near Burgh by Sands in 1307, well he also stayed here on his way up there. The night was 20th September 1306, just over a week or so before he arrived at Lanercost Priory, which just shows how slow travel was in those days, and the Thirlwall family are said to have taken great honour in entertaining him here, although we can take this with a pinch of salt as they probably had to say that. In reality, it was very costly to entertain and feed a passing king and his sizeable entourage, but in those days, they really had no choice. Luckily, he only stayed for a few nights before moving on, which was probably a relief to them all. I bet they were even more relieved when they undoubtedly later found out that he spent around 5 months at Lanercost, at considerable expense, and realized what a narrow escape they'd had.

Lastly, before we leave, you might want to have a snoop around for some buried treasure in these very parts. In the days of border raids between England and Scotland, one such raid apparently prompted the resident dwarf to jump into a well with the Lord's golden table in order to stop it falling into enemy hands. It hasn't been found yet and may well still be around here somewhere. You never know.

We rejoined the path and headed up a hill with a ditch on our right, which suggested we were still on the course of the wall. The weather was closing in on us, and I considered putting my wet gear on but settled for my hat for now. I took a moment to look back from where we had come and enjoyed the view of the valley which we had climbed out of, and from here it was easy to see the route of the vallum just south of Gilsland, which was a very prominent feature thereabouts.

As we got to the top of the hill, we were delighted to be able to see the undulating crags and hills ahead of us, which seemed to offer a glimpse of some of the wilder parts of the countryside and therefore the wall. The rain started to fall properly now, which meant that we all changed rather quickly into our wet gear, and we plodded on, alone on the hill with no one in sight other than ourselves. The ditch to our right became more pronounced as we climbed, and the overall view got better as we did so as well.

Sheep scattered ahead of us and stood nervously waiting as we passed, and after a while, we came to a minor road where we found Walltown Quarry and decided to stop for some lunch, although it was a somewhat early one. The picnic benches were wet, but we sat down anyway and enjoyed a brief respite from the rain, which had more or less stopped at this point, and we made use of the facilities too.

After a few minutes, we were ready to move on, because as soon as we stopped, we started to feel the cold. It is surprising how quickly you get warm when you get walking, but the opposite is also true, especially when you are wet.

We followed a neat path around a small lake and noticed that there were considerably more people around here. This is probably because of the car park, and it always makes me wonder how far most people are actually prepared to walk away from their cars at places like this, with the answer probably being less than you might think.

The path was pleasantly flat for a while, but after we went through a gate, a sharp left turn led us straight up a steep hill. On our left was a dry-stone wall as well as a fantastic view, but after a few hundred feet the dry-stone wall morphed back into Hadrian's Wall, though I never actually spotted the point where it did so, it was just suddenly there once again.

We followed the crest of the hill sticking close to the wall, and had a wonderful view of Kielder Forest to the north, although the cloud occasionally hid it away from us.

Suddenly and without warning, Rob slipped on a rock and went crashing down to the floor, so I did the obvious thing and grabbed my camera. He didn't look too injured, but he was very wet and looked like he had landed in something that a sheep with a poorly stomach had left behind. He didn't look too amused with me as I clicked away, but I reminded him of the historical importance of getting pictures of each other as we went head over heels.

The path now began to go up and down small hills; these Romans had been serious about this straight-line thing apparently, which at least added a bit of variety but was tiring on the knees. Once or twice I nearly slipped on the wet rocks underfoot and nearly suffered the same fate as Rob, but just managed to stop myself at the crucial moment, much to the disappointment of my mates.

The wall at this point was pretty impressive and relatively intact, or at least the lower part was. Just as I was thinking about how impressive it was, it disappeared almost into the ground and was just no more, without any apparent reason or explanation. Whether locals had robbed the bricks from this point or whether it had simply collapsed or was buried, it was impossible to say.

We continued eastwards, with crags and a long drop to our left, and the rain stopped and started once again but never really turned into much. We stopped to check our map to try and figure out exactly where we were, as we could see some stonework, and figured we were at turret 44B. King Arthur's Well was also marked as being at this point, so we all got excited and went hunting for Excalibur, but found just a boggy wet mess which made our socks wet.

We were now walking along the Roman Military Way, which was slightly set back from the wall, and the going was pretty good. The ups and downs continued, although the wall did not, and we now found ourselves walking alongside a dry-stone wall, which was the best that this area could offer.

It was steady going, though a bit monotonous, and we were pleased when we came to a small wood, which at least offered a change of scenery. This was Cockmount Hill, though the wood was very short-lived and soon brought us back out in the open to a farm which probably had one of the best views in the area, with a wide-sweeping expanse to the south. We could clearly see the course of the vallum once again a few hundred feet to the south, which seemed very distinct at this point. If you look carefully, the hillside here has been made into little terraces for farming, and as they all face south, I wonder to myself if they were once used for growing grapes.

This is a serious question. Records show that the Romans grew grapes almost two thousand years ago, and I can't imagine that they just ate them as fruit when we can all agree that there is a much better purpose for them. After the Romans left, the grape growing seems to have died out, not because us Brits were a bit rubbish with vines although we probably were, but because it was a bit chilly in the dark ages, hence the name, before the warm weather made a bit of a resurgence sometime later. So, the terraces may well have been used for this exact purpose. Measurement of tree rings back this up, also suggesting it was a bit warmer when the Romans were here, too. If growing grapes up here sounds a bit too farfetched, there is now a thriving vineyard in North Yorkshire, just near Malton, which is only around 50 miles south of the wall when measured latitudinally, so there you go. Whether the Romans managed to bottle a nice Britannia Nouveau this far north is not known, but they certainly had several vineyards further south, without a doubt.

We plodded on and after a half-mile or so we came to a farm and the site of Great Chesters Fort, according to the map. On the ground, though, there was little other than a boundary wall to see, so we didn't really stop for a look. We should be in for a treat for the next few miles, though, as there should be a lot more wall to see, and this should continue at least as far as Housesteads Fort.

This part of the wall is now known as the Clayton Wall, in recognition of the great efforts that antiquarian John Clayton went to in order to restore and preserve it, and we will learn more about him later, though it is worth noting that Clayton Wall is relatively easy to spot. It is a dry-stone reconstruction, with turf on top, and it is the lack of mortar that makes it easy to identify.

After this, a long and gradual downhill walk led us to a road where we crossed a small bridge and found another little picnic spot, where we gladly took the chance to rest our legs. I had eaten most of my lunch by now, so scavenged food from the others, and was quite successful doing so, bagging a pork pie and a snickers bar.

This was Cawfield Quarry, and I was surprised to see that there was somewhere for electric cars to charge. I've had one for a couple of years now, and have decided that I would never go back to an internal combustion engine, not even if you paid me. Actually, if you've got a serious offer, then I might consider it, but you know what I mean. It is so smooth to drive and so cheap to use, I can't understand why everyone doesn't get one. Mine wasn't even all that expensive, as it was second hand when I bought it, so I can highly recommend it. Anyway, I digress.

Finishing our second lunch of the day, it was time to move on. This quarry was similar to the previous one at Walltown, so once again we plodded around the lake and then went up a steep hill. According to the sign at the top of the hill, we were at Milecastle 42, and I have got to say that the ruins here were much better than most we had seen. The wall from this point was also very impressive and continuous, and we could see it zig-zagging up the hill ahead of us for quite some distance.

There seemed to be more people about now too, possibly because it was much later in the day but possibly also because the wall was much better here. The ups and downs continued, which was beginning to get to us all it has to be said, and I think our pace had slowed as a result.

For a while I think I went into a kind of trance, just concentrating on putting one foot in front of the other, and probably staring at the floor most of the time, which is a shame considering the amazing view. I came out of it at Caw Gap, only because we had to cross a road there, and I realized I had not taken much notice of the last couple of miles.

We had all spread out as well and had been walking along with hundreds of feet between us, so I waited here for everyone else to catch up. After five minutes, though, when nobody arrived, I realized I was probably the one at the back, so carried on.

The path up the next hill felt like the steepest so far, and I was dismayed when I got to the top of it to see that it was going to be repeated more or less immediately, although I did see Rob up ahead. Once again, the ups and downs continued for a couple of cycles, and then it just turned into one continuous upward climb.

This was because we were heading up Windshields Crags, which was going to be the highest point on this walk, something that I didn't need to read off a map as my legs and feet were already telling me this. I put my head down and just carried on moving forwards one step at a time and went back into my trance for a while, on the hope that when I once again looked up, I would be at the top.

When I did finally look up, after what seemed an age, I was nowhere near the top, which was very disappointing, to say the least. Once again, putting my head down, I trudged on, and it was a trudge because I was sick of this now. After far too long, I finally spotted the others waiting for me at the top of the hill, where they had all sat down next to the trig point which marked the summit.

I joined them for a quick rest and a nibble on some Kendal Mint Cake, as I reckoned I needed all the help I could get at the moment, and figured the others did as well. They looked as beaten as me, and I could have quite happily have sat there all day, as could they, probably.

We carried on in silence, having long since abandoned any conversation about the amazing views or how impressive the wall was, and remained silent as we slowly descended the hill and found ourselves near to Steel Rigg car park, where we wished we had parked.

After this, the path was up again, then down, and so on in an almost torturous manner. We passed the amazing ruins of Milecastle 39A without so much as batting an eyelid, never mind reaching for a camera, but where we arrived next did make us stop in our tracks because it was awesome.

Whichever direction you approach Sycamore Gap from, you are looking down on it from above. The name is obvious when you see it, with a lone sycamore tree standing in a gap between the hills.

It has of course been made famous by its starring role in the 1991 movie Robin Hood Prince of Thieves, with scenes filmed here among other places and starring movie giants Kevin Costner as Robin and Morgan Freeman as his esteemed friend Azeem. In the movie, Costner had been on the Crusades, and when he returned to England, for some indiscernible reason he travelled from the white cliffs of Dover to Nottingham via Hadrian's Wall, so we can only assume he had been gone so long, he completely forgot his way around England, or maybe he had just missed the place and wanted to take the scenic route.

I've watched this film, and it is possible, if you are a bit of a geek like I am, to pause the movie and to figure out exactly where Costner stands when Morgan Freeman is asking him which way is east when he wishes to pray. I can tell you one thing, too, Costner lies, or maybe just doesn't know, as he actually points south-west and not east at all, the fool.

Furthermore, both Freeman and Costner can be seen running up and down on the actual wall, so if the old man from Birdoswald had seen them, he would have well and truly gone nuts, and then let his dog pee up it.

By the way, while you are here, how old do you reckon that tree is? 20? 40? 60 years? Well, it is ancient and is many hundreds of years old, so be nice to it.

This tree is probably both the most photographed place and tree in Northumberland, which I can personally attest to, as I know we all took around a hundred pictures of it in between annoying tourists getting in the way. We wander off eastwards, photo-bombing a young couple as we pass, and carry on along our merry way, which is inevitably upwards.

Highshield Crags led us above the waters of Crag Lough, to which it would have been all too easy to fall to a splashy death, and as we follow the path, we are astonished to see a toddler way ahead of her parents and perilously close to the cliff edge. I am all for allowing kids a bit of independence. Still, I thought this a bit too libertarian for my liking, as did Rob. He mentioned to the parents quite tactfully that the path got narrower up ahead and if they didn't want their little angel toppling off a mountain, then they might want to get organized and put her on a lead or something. He meant well, but the parents clearly did not appreciate the advice, which was obvious from the looks on their faces.

Just to the south of here, but unfortunately not on our own personal route, is Vindolanda, one of the more famous of all the Roman forts. I had been a couple of years ago and had been fascinated by the fact that they are still digging the place up, right before your eyes. Unfortunately, no amazing discoveries were made during my visit, but you never know.

The ruins at Vindolanda are as good as, or even better than, almost any place along the wall, so it is well worth a look. Amazingly, one of the earlier accounts of the site states that the military bath-house still possessed a part of its roof as late as 1702, which is an amazing 1,500 years after it was built, give or take.

There was a famous discovery made there

a few years ago, and this was the Vindolanda Tablets. Amazingly, these were basically a load of wooden postcards, and I wondered how they had managed to survive the centuries up here in what can be, at times, an incredibly bleak environment. The reason is the soil, apparently, which has a low oxygen content and thus serves to preserve wooden postcards, shoes, bodies, boxing gloves and whatever else you want to put in the ground, so is probably not the best place to consider if you are some kind of crazed murderer intent of getting rid of your mortal enemies.

I mentioned boxing gloves because that is exactly what they found here in 2017, a nice pair of Roman boxing gloves, though it was not apparently a matching pair, which is a shame. Many shoes have also been found here, as leather lasts a particularly long time in this type of soil, apparently. Archaeologist Dr Robin Birley, who was in charge of excavations at Vindolanda for many years until he died in 2018, once famously said he was sick of the sight of them and hoped never to see another Roman shoe, boot, sandal or slipper ever again, for as long as he lived, that often was he pulling them out of the ground. There are hundreds on display at Vindolanda, and for every one that you can see, there are dozens more in the storeroom, apparently.

Another interesting find dates back to 2014, when Birley and his team discovered, wait for it, oh, I wish I had a drum roll, they discovered the only known example of a wooden Roman toilet seat. The BBC made big news of this at the time, and when you see the thing, it is definitely and instantly recognizable for what it is. It was discovered in a muddy trench which had previously been filled with, well, I will let you use your imagination there. Birley described it as very well made and fairly comfortable looking, and he stated that he is now searching for the toilet that went with it, with him apparently getting rather excited about it on the basis that it could be full of astonishing artefacts. He is probably right, because when you think about it if you dropped your ring or necklace or a chihuahua down a toilet that had been shared with fifty men, how likely are you to go down there and get it?

The toilets really were shared too and were often a place where people would go to hang out. Those crazy Romans would sit and chat while they did their business, which all sounds a bit weird, but it gets worse. They obviously had no toilet paper but would use a sponge on a stick instead. The thing is, and I'm terribly sorry about this, but the stick was shared too. They even had a toilet god, Crepitus, who was also the god of flatulence, seriously, as well as a sewer goddess, Cloacina, and finally a god of poop, Stercutius. They were obsessed and had gods for everything.

Back to the tablets, though. Perhaps the most famous of them, number 291, tells the story of how the wife of the commander of a nearby fort, who was called Claudia Severa, invited the wife of the commander of Vindolanda, Sulpicia Lepidina, to her birthday party. Such awesome names.

Another one confirms that the Romans had a derogatory nickname for the locals, and that was Brittunculi, which basically meant *little Britons*, which is pretty funny when you think about it.

My own personal favourite, however, is the story of how the handwriting on some of the tablets that were discovered in 2017 matched the handwriting on some discovered way back in 1992. The earlier batch consisted of around 800 tablets and included some very informal messages. Two stand out above all of the others, though. One of them simply states *Send Beer*, while the other complains about the state of the roads around these parts. Some things never change.

Either fortunately or unfortunately, these are regarded as treasures of national importance, so some of them have been sent to the British Museum down in London, which if you remember, is the one designed by Sir Robert Smirke. There are, however, plenty still to see at Vindolanda.

Tall trees gave us a canopy as we moved on, which was great, but their roots tried to trip us up for the next mile or so, and nearly succeeded. A climb over a wall was therefore welcomed when it led us into an open field and a smoother path, and we found ourselves constantly heading downhill for a while, which was also good.

All too soon, though, we were heading up a very long, but quite high hill, past Hotbank Farm. A crowd of people had gathered halfway up the hill, and as we approached, it was clear that something was wrong. A group of young students were looking distressed, and when we got closer it was apparent that one of them had clearly had a bit of a fall and had managed to damage her ankle, and they were clearly at a loss as what to do.

Robin was straight in there, well, he is a lifeguard and first aider, and he corralled the students together so that we could organize a lift over the gate and to the farm. The farmer had also realized that something was up, and in no time at all, he had backed his Land Rover up, loaded her in, and was whisking her down the hopefully not too bumpy track towards the hospital in Haltwhistle.

The excitement was all over in two minutes flat, after which we carried on up the never-ending hill ahead of us, with adrenaline now pumping through our bodies. We once again had the wall to our left, which helped to keep the wind out of my hair, but the wall here was not high enough to shelter Robin. This didn't matter, of course, because his hair had blown away a long time ago.

Once again, the walking here seemed a lot longer than it actually was, probably because we were all completely shattered by now. This was definitely turning out to be the hardest day, due to a combination of the distance and the landscape, which was basically one hill after another.

Coming to a sign that directed the Pennine Way walkers to the north, we continued east and knew we must be nearing Housesteads Fort, where we would take a well-earned rest. Just before Housesteads, we came to Milecastle 37, which was pretty impressive compared to some other milecastles, which were barely visible. This one is one that had clearly had the Clayton treatment, and in fact, has the tallest section of the wall that was restored by him, and sure enough, there is no mortar holding the stones together.

Just a few minutes later, we arrived at Housesteads, where almost immediately we found ourselves resting our bums on some rocks and having a good long rest. Anthony had arrived here way before the rest of us and was already looking refreshed even as we sat down.

As I looked around, I decided it would be impossible to tell whether or not this fort was better than Birdoswald. It was very similar in layout, size and remains, and if you looked at the ruins you could clearly see that the Romans knew a thing or two about central heating and running water, but you could also see all of that at Birdoswald. I don't like to sit on fences, though, so I got a coin out, and can therefore now authoritatively tell you that without doubt, in no uncertain terms, that Housesteads is absolutely the much better one of the two. Probably.

This fort, however, has something that others lack. It has one of the best-preserved latrines of the Roman Empire, which is certainly saying something. What's more, it wasn't just local troops that would have used it. Soldiers came from far and wide to Housesteads, including some who had travelled all the way from Syria, which makes you wonder what they would have thought when they got here. Hopefully, they would have arrived in July and not in January.

After this, we put our heads down for the long slog up Sewingshields Crags, passing through the King's Wicket, which sounds exciting but is actually just a gate. It is alternately called Busy Gap, and in the field on the left are some earthworks that help to explain why. We must remember that there were not as many holes in the wall in centuries gone by, but this is at least one place that seems to have bucked the trend. Bandits and raiders would use this place to get through the wall, often with stolen cattle, and would sometimes hold their cattle in these enclosures, which would, of course, have been more complete way back then. The people that utilized the area were called Busy Gap Rogues, and may well have been the same families who became the cross-border Reivers.

It seemed never-ending, but when we finally got to the trig point at the top, we knew we were nearly done, so to speak. As a bonus, the sun finally decided to make an appearance, so with a renewed sense of vitality, we carried on knowing that we could not have far to go. We were treated to another section of the wall which popped up out of the ground, followed by the foundations of a turret, with the map telling us it was turret 35A, which confirmed that we were definitely counting down. Rob then pointed out the rather large information board that I had somehow missed as I fumbled with my map, that had 35A in rather large letters too, it had to be said, and he said all of this with more than a hint of sarcasm, the swine.

The wall was intermittent after this, once again presumably buried for its own good, and the path continued to snake up and down the small hills along the way. I had heard it described by others that the wall was a rock and mortar scar across the landscape, which it was, although everywhere that it appeared, it was a beautiful scar, and in no way ugly.

I stopped at the next milecastle to empty my shoes of stones, which I had meant to do for a while but just hadn't bothered with, and when I took my shoes off, I realized I had more than a couple of blisters. I was a bit worried, then, when I failed to locate any blister plasters in my bag, and had to beg some from Anthony, who proffered them at only £5 apiece. He was joking, of course, or at least I hoped he was.

It was little comfort, then, when we finally found ourselves heading downhill, because the path just seemed to go on and on, with no end in sight. It led us through another small wood and past the rear of a farm, which was perilously close to a long, steep drop, and where one misstep could end very badly indeed. On the plus side, if this happened it would mean not having to walk any further, I mused to myself.

Perhaps it was psychological, but it seemed like it took us hours to get down that hill, and when we finally hit the road at the bottom, just past a sign that said we were at Milecastle 34, we were absolutely worn out. We walked the last mile or so to the car and were that tired we didn't even move out of the way of the traffic speeding past. Changing into our comfy shoes, we did the usual thing and went to pick the van up before heading back to the campsite.

We couldn't be bothered to cook, so we stopped at the fish and chip shop in Haltwhistle and grabbed some food, which we brought back to eat outside of our tents. The sun had remained out, and it was quite a pleasant evening, and after our food, we all hobbled one by one to get a shower and to clean up.

It is amazing how a little bit of food and a good wash will transform you, and by around 7pm we were more or less reinvigorated. A discussion was held, and we unanimously decided to pay a visit to a nearby pub, just to support the local economy, you understand. Appropriately enough, we were soon at The Milecastle Inn just up the road and ordering four of the barman's best pints.

We came out of the pub heading for the beer garden, and the sun was still out as we passed two elderly gentlemen occupying a small bench and enjoying the evening sunshine. I think one of them took a liking to Anthony, and it is important to say that Anthony is very happily married, so this liking spooked him a bit, though it made us all laugh.

After a half-hour or so, as the sun disappeared behind the hills, we decided to relocate into the pub, which meant we had to pass these two gents again, where once again one of them made it quite clear he liked Anthony.

He hid behind us as we passed them, and then he hid in the corner once we were inside, especially when his newfound friend came inside looking for him. We were all creasing ourselves laughing at this, but Anthony was not amused, so abruptly we had no choice but to leave and head back towards the campsite and relative safety.

How we didn't get run over on the long walk back still amazes me, as the road was narrow and we were wobbly, but get back we did, and before long we were all safely tucked up in our tents with zips firmly up to protect us from zombie cats, and in Anthony's case, padlocked.

CHAPTER 5
Middle of Nowhere to Halton Shields

The day did not start well. We awoke to deafening rain battering the canvas of our tents but luckily remained dry. The weather forecast promised rain, rain, rain, and we were seriously considering a zero-day, where we would get no mileage. Unfortunately, work commitments meant that we could not stay an extra day, so this would mean missing out a section of the walk, which was not ideal, to say the least.

As we did our breakfast and got things ready, just in case, the rain got even heavier. If you have ever been camping in the rain, then you will know how deafening the sound of it can be inside your tent, but sometimes when you go outside, it seems as if it is hardly raining. Unfortunately, this was not the case today. When I popped my head outside, it was as if I had just been for a quick shower, and I had to dry my head with a towel afterwards.

We discussed our options and went from

not walking to walking and back again a couple of times. I argued that we should just go, wearing our full waterproofs, and see what happened. This argument evidently won the day, so a bit later than usual, just after 8 am, we ventured out on our not so merry way. We dropped the car off at our finish point, which was a lay-by just before Halton Shields, and then drove back to the middle of nowhere, where we would resume our walk. It was gone 9 o'clock by the time we had done this, which was late, but we figured that today would not be such a long walk in terms of both mileage and actual time taken, as it was not as hilly.

From the van, we would head east and resume the walk near Milecastle 34, and for around five miles, the route would hug the main road. There would be a brief stop at Brocolitia Fort, followed by more walking to the next village, many miles on, which was Walwick. After this, we would soon be at Chollerford, the site of Chesters Fort, another well-known fort, where we would cross the River North Tyne, which I always thought an unusual name. After Chollerford, the path would more or less continue to stick to the road and would take us through Greenfield, which did not look to be much of a village, before we would finish at Halton Shields.

With at least some trepidation because of the continuing bad weather, it is perhaps not surprising that we exited the van in a somewhat unwilling manner to start our walk. The first few miles of walking clearly set the tone for the day, which was rain, rain, rain. There was not much wall to look at either, other than the dry-stone wall to our right, and I wondered if this too had been pilfered from its older cousin. It was easy walking, however, albeit a miserable start to the day. Within thirty minutes, my feet were sodden, however, and I gave up all hope of being anything resembling dry by the time we would finish that evening.

There was not much to see in terms of bricks at all, I discovered as we moved along, and I wondered if we had seen all the wall we were going to see while we were walking yesterday. The view was not great either, due to the weather, but the countryside up here was very open, so I suspected that on a nicer day, the views would be spectacular.

The path closely followed the route of the road here, hugging it very closely, and we were once again following what had become known as General Wade's Military Road. This road would continue more or less all the way to Newcastle from here, and criminally almost all of it had been built along the route of the actual wall, as opposed to the sections we encountered earlier which had been built some distance from it. This road, therefore, is one of the main reasons why there is very little wall to be seen any more around here, as much of it now lies a few feet under the tarmac having been used as an incredibly cheap and rather handy form of hardcore. Although this would be unthinkable nowadays, I mean you try to get planning permission for anything within the site of the wall, good luck with that, it should be said that it was not entirely without controversy at the time either.

Indeed, one such wall-hugger was Peter Stukeley, a would-be archaeologist of this era who had worked at Stonehenge and Avebury, but who also ventured into the badlands of the north to study the wall. He was one of the few that recognized the importance of it and called for Wade's road to follow a different route, perhaps that of the Roman Military Way, rather than the wall itself. He described how the workers *beat the stones to pieces, to make the road withal. Every carving, inscription, altar, milestone, pillar, etc., undergoes the same vile havoc, from the hands of these wretches.* He didn't mince his words then. Unfortunately, no one listened to him, and with that, the road was built, and the wall was gone.

The rain got heavier, which I did not think possible, but we plodded on regardless. It seemed that no one else was silly enough to be out here today, so we at least had the path to ourselves, well, ourselves and several hundred sad-looking sheep, which was little comfort, to be honest.

I had put my phone in a small plastic bag, so it didn't get ruined, so when it rang, and by the time I had managed to get it out of my pocket to answer it, it was too late. My wife had tried to call, and I knew why.

Our families were due to come up that evening and spend our final couple of nights with us. I rang her back and gave her the picture of how miserable it was, and basically told her the ball was in her court. My wife, Leeanne, does not like camping you see, so there was no way I was going to drag her up here in this as I felt I might never hear the end of it. Oh, no, if she was coming up here in this weather, then she was going to do it knowing exactly what it was like. I advised her to check the weather forecast and to get back to me later that afternoon, and that if she decided she was coming, to bring a dinghy.

By the time I had finished talking to her, my hand was red raw and absolutely freezing, so I vowed that all further communication would be done by text. Shoving the phone back into the bag and into an inner pocket, I was annoyed when it buzzed a minute later and had to go through all of this again, only to learn it was a marketing call about some accident that I'd had and how much compensation I was due. I deleted the message and decided to turn it off.

A little while further on, our straight path was interrupted, which was a welcome variation, as we went around a farm. A short while later, we crossed the main road, swimming through clouds of water left by passing trucks, and headed towards the exciting-sounding Temple of Mithras, which sits behind Carrawburgh Fort. Compared to

Housesteads or Birdoswald, there is very little to see at Carrawburgh, but the temple is pretty cool, though quite small.

Mithraism is a bit of an unknown quantity when it comes to the Romans, and has variously been described as a religion or even as a cult. It must have been quite common, though, as there are also temples dedicated to it at other sites, including one in London as well as one in Rome itself. I particularly liked the rather dapper carving of a figure which was here, which reminded me of a headless leprechaun.

Next to the temple was Coventina's Well. Before the Romans arrived, a beautiful goddess lived in these parts, and this was her well, apparently. When the Romans came, they took over the well and built a square enclosure around it, and piped the water off to their fort. In return, offerings were regularly left at the site of the well and eventually a temple was built. With the withdrawal of the Romans, however, the temple was dismantled and the offerings placed carefully within the well itself, where they sat for almost 2,000 years.

Discovered by local miners, John Clayton, who was, of course, responsible for saving much of the wall we had earlier passed, was notified and he promptly excavated the site. He must have been thrilled, as he discovered an abundance of treasures and offerings, many with Coventina's name on them. Like much of what Clayton discovered, these items can now be seen on display at Chesters Roman Fort Museum.

We crossed the road once again and got back onto the wet grass with the rain still pounding down all around us. The only redeeming factor about today's walk was that it was relatively flat, compared to the ridiculous roller-coaster ride that had been yesterday. My legs were still aching from that, in particular my knees, which is surely a sign of getting old.

We continued along, following the path along the earthworks which remained distinctly lacking in the wall capacity, and ever so slowly the sky appeared to brighten a little. I would even go so far as to say that the rain eased off a little, although most assuredly did not stop.

This part of the route was also slap bang on top of the military way, which had been in use for two thousand years, and as we walked along, I wondered how many people had been along here in that time.

Somewhere near Black Carts, the wall seemed to emerge gradually from the ground, almost like a submarine surfacing, and I wondered if we had been walking over another stretch where the wall had been buried to preserve it.

It was nice to see our old friend again, although it would seem that it was only a passing visit, as after a couple of hiccups in its length it seemed to be once again gone.

A quick detour around a farm brought little

excitement, as did a venture across some fields that took us out of our way and then brought us back into the small village of Walwick. This is a nice enough village, but unfortunately, there was nothing to keep us here such as a large under-cover shopping centre or a KFC or anything else re-motely dry, so we splashed on.

We were walking along the road now, so there was little to see, at least until we got to Ches-ters Fort just outside of Chollerford. We got our little passports stamped, with the stamp being hung on the gate to stop us smelly hikers bother-ing the staff I reckoned and paddled on into the village itself.

I have since found out that this is another one of the sites where you can see a Roman willy carved into the rock. If you do go in then, head for the headquarters building, and look for a slab near to what looks like the metal grate for a circular well, and look at the larger bit of paving just next to it. It is rather obvious, trust me. If you have the time and the inclination to see yet another willy, there is one on the bathhouse too.

That is not the only reason to visit Ches-ters, though. We have already heard the name of John Clayton mentioned, and Chesters was both his family home and also the first site that he could be considered to have saved. Clayton was born in Newcastle and was trained as a lawyer, but his love lay with all things old, and old Roman stuff in particular. His father bought the big house here, which was the Chesters Estate, and included the site of the old Roman fort of the same name.

With his interest piqued, Clayton then spent the rest of his life buying up as much land as he could that was on, near or over the wall, and being a man of means, he could certainly afford to do this. By the time of his death in 1890, he owned five forts, including Chesters, Vindolanda and Housesteads, along with much of the wall in between.

He added much to the knowledge of the wall and even caused some serious rethinking of its history. When he excavated Cawfields Milecastle, for instance, he discovered a gateway to the north, which seriously questioned the old idea that the wall had solely been built to protect the south from northern barbarians, and introduced the idea that it might have been a point where taxes were collected.

He amassed so many artefacts that a purpose-built museum now houses what is called the Clayton Collection, which can be seen at Chesters, and houses over 11,000 items in addition to an amazing 12,000 coins, and can truly be said to be priceless. And did I mention that you can see a carved willy on the floor?

Clayton went on excavating sections of the wall right up until his death. He ensured his work would not stop even after his death though, leaving an absolute fortune to his nephew Nathaniel, on the proviso that *whenever an estate came into the market having on it some portion of the Wall, he strove to become its possessor.* Judging by the legacy left nowadays, it is pretty clear that Nathaniel never let his uncle down.

We carried on along the road, temporarily moving away from the course of the actual wall in order to cross the River North Tyne. Reaching the roundabout, and spotting a tearoom and café, we piled in and immediately took our wet gear off while we ordered our teas and coffees. It was good to get this gear off, as I had now begun to sweat underneath it, and judging by the slowly brightening sky outside, we might even be able to keep it off.

After we had our drinks but had not really dried off at all, it was, unfortunately, time to move on. It had, however, stopped raining by now, which was one good thing at least, but my feet were still wet, and I did not relish walking for another few hours in them but had no choice, I guess.

We crossed the narrow bridge and enjoyed the views over the river and passed a road sign that told us we had 21 miles to go to Newcastle. Shortly after this, the path ran out, and we found ourselves walking on the grass verge, which was not ideal, although we seemed to have little choice at this stage.

Going up a hill, and finding ourselves at the top of Brunton Bank, there was a small stretch of wall in the field to our right. Seeing no way into the field, and not wanting to tackle the barbed wire fence, we carried on, but then came across a sign pointing us to the way in. We followed it and doubled back to have a quick look at the wall as well as a little rest. This was Planetrees and was quite an impressive bit of wall, and possibly one of the last stretches of it that we would be seeing, as it was a bit thin on the ground from now on apparently. How this bit had survived is a mystery, but here it was. This bit of wall is also one of the places where the building of the wall changed. Although the base here is the original wide version at 10 feet, the wall built onto this foundation is from here on narrower at 8 feet, which is clearly visible if you look down.

We had a good look at it and enjoyed a little rest, before moving on once again, where we found ourselves gradually going up a hill, but it was a steady climb and nothing like yesterday. The grass verge did narrow as we went along, though, which became an issue. I wondered where the proper path had gone and how we had missed it, but it was too late now, and none of us was willing to double back to find it anyway. This did mean, however, that we had to keep stopping every time a car or truck came along. When a bus approached, we actually had to insert ourselves into the hedge. Still, we made slow and steady progress until we finally came to a small lay-by that had a worryingly large wooden cross.

I wondered if this was the site of some accident, where people decide to build shrines in memory of their loved ones, but it was not. It was, in fact, the marker for the location of the Battle of Heavenfield, which was admittedly not a battle I had heard of. This was probably because it happened a very long time ago and involved the Welsh, which I do not mean in a nasty way, but you surely get my point. Anyway, the original cross that was erected on this site was said to cause miracles for anyone who got a splinter from it, which makes me wonder if King Edward Longshanks kept a bit of it with his thorn from Christ's crown. Anyway, it is not surprising that the original is no longer here, and presumably, in fact, vanished astonishingly quickly I would imagine, due to its promise of miracles.

A little while further, we managed to get back onto the path, which was a relief and meant we were no longer at risk of becoming roadkill. There was still little sign of the wall though; however, there was an impressive ditch which we walked along for some time.

The weather was playing nice for us as well, which is good because I received a text message from my wife telling me that they were going to risk it and were on their way up. Be it on her head, I thought. I had also received a message from Rob in Jamaica, asking what our weather was like, along with a picture of a sandy beach and a blue sky, and guessed he knew full well what our weather was like having probably checked our weather forecast. I had earlier taken a picture of the phallus that had been carved in the wall, which I for-warded to him, and hoped he would get my point.

At some point, we crossed the road, which was quite frankly the most exciting thing that had happened for some time, and went through a small wood before emerging in a field full of cow-pats. Continuing along, we saw the odd bits of brick, but it was hard to say if they were Roman or not. After a couple more miles, we arrived at somewhere much more interesting, which was the Errington Arms, a pub which also doubled as a coffee house, apparently.

Of course, we all went in, and I had a fabu-lous hot chocolate with all the trimmings, includ-ing cream and marshmallows. It was awesome. Looking at the map, we only had a short distance to go now, and it was an easy decision to say that today had been far easier than yesterday. Still, the downside is that it had also been far less interest-ing, particularly because of the lack of wall and the lack of anything along this stretch really. Still, it had been a nice walk, although a somewhat wet one, and would probably have been one that went through beautiful countryside had we been able to see anything, although of course, we could not.

Now would be a good time to talk about Corbridge, which was just a couple of miles to the south of here. I think its Roman name had been Constipatium or something like that, and it was a very important place in the Roman world. It was the most northerly town in the Roman Empire, and stood at the junction of Stanegate, which if you have been paying attention you will know runs across the north of England east to west, while Dere Street, which started at York running north, passed through here and went all the way through the badlands of Scotland as far north as the Antonine Wall. Indeed, the road that this tea-room was on was also the route of Dere Street heading north, and it would have crossed Ha-drian's Wall here at the Port Gate. This is a modern name for a fortified gate that allowed travellers, traders and anyone else to be physically stopped and checked before moving through the wall, and possibly relieved of some coin. Although nobody knows for sure what it looked like, it is thought to have resembled Arbeia, which is a reconstruction of a fort at South Shields, and if it did look like this, it would have been very intimidating to all who passed through.

Corbridge is also home to the famous Steve Bruce, who in his time has managed Newcastle United, Sunderland Town, and of course my own favourite, Hull City, but don't hold that against him, as he's a very nice man indeed. Catherine Cookson also came from the place, who of course sold tens of millions of books, and for a long time, her books were the most borrowed ones from libraries, though Jacqueline Wilson eventually took the top spot from her, but only after Cookson had been dead for four years.

Anyway, like I said, Corbridge was a very

important place for the Romans, and although its exact name is not known, the Vindolanda tablets, which we discussed earlier, referred to its shortened name of Coria, so at least we have a clue. It is probably one of the most excavated places in Britain, if not the world, and work has been ongoing here since before the First World War. If you do visit, as I did a while back, you can go and see an actual part of where the Stanegate ran into the town that formed its eastern terminus. Stanegate is slightly different from most Roman roads in one particular aspect. While Roman roads traditionally ran in straight lines, bulldozing their way through peoples' houses and going straight up and down steep hills, Stanegate was different in that it followed the course of least resistance, perhaps because it was built well before Hadrian's Wall.

There is a lot more to see in Corbridge than just stone, though. In the museum, there are coins, tablets and trinkets, and even something described as a conical flask, but to me looks like some kind of Roman bong, and before you dismiss this, the Romans were known for their parties and knew exactly how to get high. One of their favourite methods was to eat an aptly named Dreamfish. This was their equivalent to LSD, and after a couple of hours of having eaten it, you would get hallucinations of the most bizarre kind. Unfortunately, what goes up must come down, so you would then get a good few days' worth of the worst kind of nightmares, possibly about zombie cats. They also made widespread use of opium, and in the 2nd century, Marcus Aurelius, the last of the good emperors, wrote a book called *Meditations*, probably because he was constantly as high as a kite.

They even had their own morning-after pill, of sorts. Made from an extract of the Silphium plant, which was incredibly rare, impossible to cultivate, and only grew in the wild in a very small part of what is now Libya, the locals guarded their fields vigorously. Unfortunately, possibly due to over-farming or a changing climate, Silphium went extinct sometime during the reign of Emperor Nero. Possibly expecting him to use his finest wise men and scientists to somehow manage to re-cultivate the plant and therefore save it forever, the Silphium farmers went to some lengths to collect and transport the last known example of their precious plant, delivering it to Emperor Nero himself. They were probably somewhat surprised and maybe even a little disappointed then when he had it for his dinner.

Why it didn't grow when cultivated is a mystery, but two modern-day examples may shed light on this conundrum. Poppy seeds only start to grow when they are exposed to light and therefore tend to prefer disturbed soil. If you think about it, this is why we now associate poppies with the First World War battlefields of Europe, where the soil was surely disturbed in the most extreme sense of the word.

There is also the case of the huckleberry. This tart red berry native to North America's National Parks is added to everything from jam to ice-cream, and there is never enough to go around. Incredibly brave or extremely crazy Americans, I'll let you decide, risk life and limb against bears collecting this stuff, that's right, I said bears, and despite serious efforts to cultivate it that have gone on for over a hundred years, it has still eluded even the most proficient botanist's capabilities to do so. Apparently, the only way to grow them is to chop some trees down near an existing patch of the plant, and simply wait, hopefully with a big gun in your hands in case a bear comes along wanting a snack. I would have no chance growing silphium or huckleberries, as I can't even grow a cactus, which let's face it, manage to grow in some of the most inhospitable places on earth, apart from when I'm nearby. The bears would probably get me, too.

Anyway, after we had finished our drinks, we trundled along once again, still with wet feet, and carried on eastwards. We found a path running alongside the road but behind some trees and a wall, which at least meant we were off the road, and the next and last mile of the walk was possibly the nicest mile of the day, as the sun came out once and for all, which really lifted our spirits.

Jumping in the car, in no time at all we were back in the middle of nowhere, where we picked up the van, before heading back to the campsite to clean up before the women got there because if they saw us in the state we were in, they would go nuts.

It was only a few minutes drive back to the campsite from the van, and we all hurried around to get cleaned up before the families arrived. I was actually in the shower when I became aware that my children must be around, as I heard the explosions and the gunshots and the screams. This was, of course, my son, who was playing one violent game or another on his phone while he wandered past the shower block.

I dried myself and went outside to find that, yes, everyone was here, and they were already starting to put another tent up. Apparently, the ladies and the children were sleeping in their own tent, as for some unfathomable reason, they did not wish to share canvas with us, their cherished loved ones. While us men may be generally known to make odd noises through the night, I still thought this a tad rude, especially as they had decided to pitch their tent about as far away from us as possible and at the other end of the campsite. They variously claimed that it was because they wanted electric hook ups, or to be near the toilet blocks in case of any early hours desire for their use, or because they didn't want the long trek up the hill. We knew full well, however, that it was because they wanted a full night's sleep without the possibility of any strange night-time noises, or even worse, smells.

With the tents up, we all jumped into the cars; we had three of them now and drove into Haltwhistle for some fish and chips. It was pleasant in the market square as we ate our hearty meal until that is, we were bombarded by wasps. More accurately, I think it was one psychopathic wasp, which went around us all one by one. It did finally meet its end, though, when it flew into Chris' can of coke, and after nearly having swallowed it, he spat it out and danced on it for a good few minutes, and that was the end of that.

I am a notoriously fast eater, so while the others slowly finished their food, I wandered off to have a quick look at the church behind the shops, but it was all locked up, so I was back in just a few minutes, after which we all jumped back into the cars and went back to the campsite.

Forming a circle of chairs just outside our tent, and having made the women climb the hill, the kids were having fun playing games and running around. The pigs were staring at us through the gap in the fence, and following a conversation about our washing habits that week, my wife asked me if the pigs were related. *In-laws*, I replied.

Quite late on, possibly around 9 pm, a young family turned up and clumsily put their tent up, which amused us considerably, if only for a short while. We had some music on low and enjoyed a couple of drinks, and spent most of the evening chatting about this and that, as well as making plans for tomorrow. The idea was to drop a car off on the outskirts of Newcastle, just near the A1, and ask the ladies nicely if they would then drop us back off at Halton Shields, where we would resume our walk. They reluctantly agreed, bless them, although it did take a glass or two of vino before they finally said yes.

At around 10 pm, just as we were getting ready to pack everything up and go to sleep, a young boy came across from the family that had pitched the late tent and said that his mum had asked if we could please shut up as they had a young baby. We looked at each other, thinking that we hadn't really been making much noise anyway, but assured the youngster that we would, indeed, shut up.

After that, we very quietly went to sleep, but unfortunately, several times in fact throughout the night, we experienced piercing and chilling audible reminders that the young family did indeed have a very young, and very noisy baby, though baby what, I am not sure. By the sounds of it, it could have been a hyena, or maybe perhaps a howler monkey, it was hard to tell.

CHAPTER 6

Halton Shields to Newburn

Breakfast took a little longer than usual, as we were cooking for the five thousand today, or at least that's what it felt like. Before long, though, we were ready to go, and the ladies were going to follow us in the people carrier to Newburn, on the outskirts of Newcastle, where we were leaving Anthony's car, and they would then drop us back at Halton Shields. We stopped at the kitchen block to top up on water, however, and got talking to the manager Steve, and thought we had best apologize for any noise we made the previous night which had disturbed the young family camped near us, as they were, of course, his customers. He looked a bit puzzled and said there shouldn't be a family up there. He added that the reason he had put us up there, was so that we could make a noise and not disturb the families, who were, or at least should be, all at the bottom of the camp, funnily enough in the family area.

It was a surprisingly short drive to the

outskirts of Newcastle, thanks be to those nice straight Roman roads once again, and after what seemed like no time at all, we had dropped Anthony's car off and were on the way back to Halton Shields. We stopped briefly in the lay-by, bade the ladies farewell, and set off on our way.

It was refreshingly dry this morning, though there was a fair bit of cloud. I actually preferred walking under a nice, thick layer of the finest British cloud though, because it obviously helped you to keep cooler for longer.

For a while, we walked on the grass verge, which soon developed into a footpath adjacent to the road, until finally becoming a footpath all on its own and moved pleasantly away from the road and the speeding traffic that it carried. A line of trees on our left obscured the view to the north, but to the south, we saw an endless expanse of cultivated fields, dotted with the occasional sprinkling of trees, all at their August finest.

After a couple of miles, the path crossed over to the other side of the road, before taking us on a little diversion around a field just for the fun of it. This meant that we missed the village of Wallhouses, which presumably described the origin of the bricks used to build them, but as we didn't actually see any, it is impossible to say. Anthony was on form at this point and was well ahead of the rest of us, and I was at the back mostly.

The vallum ran parallel with the road just

to the south along this stretch, but there was no apparent sign of it, and certainly no sign of the wall, but then there wouldn't be if they had used it all to build the village, I guess. At this point, the path followed a route through some trees, which was pleasant enough at this time of the morning, with the birds being still pretty chirpy.

Surprisingly, we then stumbled across a pub, literally, as I nearly went over on my ankles due to not paying attention, and more surprisingly still, the pub was open.

This was the Robin Hood Inn, and because of the name of the pub, it was only right that Robin got the round in. Going inside, we were the only customers, which is not surprising at all given the early hour. Normally we wouldn't go into a pub mid-morning, but this was one of the points where you get your little Hadrian's Wall Passport stamped, so we had no choice, I mean, they practically forced us in.

Rob got us all a drink, which was neither a half-pint nor a pint but was, in fact, two-thirds of a pint. I had never had two-thirds of a pint before, so this was a bit of a novelty but was just the right amount for a mid to late morning treat. We chatted idly to the landlady for a while, and she told us all about her pub, and we all enjoyed ourselves immensely. As we came out of the pub, we got our stamp, which was actually stored in a box outside next to the door. Technically we hadn't needed to enter the pub, but, well, you know, supporting local businesses and all that.

We were soon on our way, complete with stamps in book, and the road carried on as straight as before. As we left the pub, I noted that it too was of very solid construction, and wondered if the name of the pub was due to the fact that they had robbed the bricks to build it. I wish I had asked, but there was no way I was going back. One thing puzzled me, though. There was a *beware of trains* sign on the wall.

We chatted among ourselves as we sauntered along, still more or less at the beginning of what was hopefully going to be quite an easy day, and the weather was improving by the hour.

For the next couple of miles, the straight road led us slowly but surely through a landscape that offered little variation, other than a couple of small reservoirs near Harlow Hill. This was Wade's Military Road at its finest, and I wondered once again what treasures were buried beneath it.

Just north of Harlow Hill is an old airfield, although we couldn't see it, but it has some interesting stories to tell. RAF Ouston was built at the outset of the Second World War, although quite bizarrely and quite possibly uniquely for an RAF base, they nearly built it in the wrong place by accident. When Air Ministry officials in London sent a delegation north to inspect the site, someone presumably pulled out a road map of England and promptly went to a completely different Ouston, some twenty-odd miles away at the other side of

Hexham.

Finally discovering their mistake, they eventually ended up in the right place and set about building their base despite some local opposition. It opened in 1941, and featured a Roman helmet on its badge, as a nod to some of the archaeology that had presumably been destroyed when building it. Many squadrons based here repeatedly failed to score any kills, and the base developed something of a reputation, which was not entirely a positive one. Ironically, therefore, its motto was *Persist*.

This was perhaps the correct motto, as exampled by 226 Squadron RAF, who managed to crash three of their planes on their first day stationed at the base. After the war, the runway was extended just in case we needed to ever go and bomb those pesky Russians, which thankfully never happened. This meant that the most exciting thing that ever happened here, then, was motor racing, which took advantage of those incredibly long runways. Indeed, none other than Jackie Stewart won his first-ever race here, driving en E-Type Jaguar, and of course, he went on to become a world champion and was given the short nickname of the Flying Scot, when someone pointed out that the name Flying Scotsman had already accidentally been given to a train so was no longer available.

We reached the end of this stretch as we arrived at Heddon-on-the Wall, which was a welcome relief after these miles of boredom. We crossed over the dual carriageway that we had driven along earlier in the day, and a left turn took us along a pasture with apparently thousands of sheep within it.

A right turn at the Three Tuns Pub saw us in the village properly, but there was no sign of Anthony at all, who had once again gone ahead of us a little earlier. This was a concern, as we didn't know which way he had gone or if he even knew the route of the walk. A phone call went straight to his voice mail, and a text message went unanswered. We decided to sit in the park for a few minutes in case Anthony rang us back, and I took the opportunity to go and have a look at the church, which was open, so I went inside and sat down for a while.

It was nice and cool inside, and you could clearly see the original stones of the church, which were once again pilfered from the wall. There is quite a big bit of the wall left in the village, though, which was quite surprising. It is in a field at the eastern end of Towne Gate and is where I went next.

When I got there, I was surprised once more about the quantity of wall that was left and wondered why it had not been nicked. Perhaps the locals around here were more honest. It's worth a look, as this particular bit of the wall was built to the original specification of 10 feet wide before they decided to reduce it to only 8 feet wide later on, as we saw earlier at Planetrees.

I took a couple of pictures and wandered back to the others expecting to see Anthony by now, but when I got there, there was still no sign of him, and a further phone call and text went as unanswered as the previous ones. We did the only thing we could do under the circumstances and carried on walking.

Heading south through the village, the road began to gradually drop down what looked like a large valley, with a glimpse of the River Tyne down below us through the trees. Once we were at the bottom of the valley, we would be following the river for the rest of the day, in fact for the rest of the walk, so we could only hope that we would bump into Anthony down there somewhere. We weren't necessarily worried about him at this stage, it's just that he had the car keys.

The houses gave way to the fields, and one of the last ones had a sign saying *Slow Children Playing*, and I wondered if they meant the children were slow or if they wanted you to drive slowly, I mean, you never know nowadays. People really should think carefully before putting signs up. For instance, I once saw a sign that said *shoot the kids, hang the family, frame the wife*, and it wasn't until I realized it was in a photographer's window that I breathed a sigh of relief.

Frivolities aside, we entered a small wood, which was refreshingly cool, and a left turn soon had us heading down the hill and towards a golf club, apparently. It was one of those ultra-posh ones, with lots of nice cars parked outside, along with a couple of golf buggies, which I figured would help us finish this walk in no time if we stole one.

We walked on though, not wishing to clash with the law at this late stage, and followed the path next to a ridiculously high brick wall with very good security, judging by the cameras watching us pass. We mused as to what was on the other side of the wall, and I suggested a body farm, though I think it was just the golf club.

We then had to duck and dive across the golf course itself, which thankfully proved to be a non-event, despite the multitudes of people who were out knocking balls left, right and centre, by the looks of it. On the way across, we met a couple of hikers coming the other way, and we asked them if they had seen a chubby old bloke walking by himself, probably chain-smoking, and they said they had, so at least now we knew that Anthony wasn't lying dead in a ditch somewhere. Again, this isn't any kind of compassion or anything, we just kept thinking of those lovely car keys.

Finally at the river bank, and walking east along the River Tyne, we felt as if we were nearing the end of today's walk, although, in reality, we still had a few miles to go. Had we gone west, however, it would only be a short walk to Wylam, which is where George Stephenson was born, and if you are not sure who I am on about, this is the guy that built one of the earliest, and certainly one of the most famous trains ever, *The Rocket,* and who became known as the *Father of the Railways*. It seems that wherever I go in our little country, I keep finding links to him, but I guess he was just prolific in his time. Just half a mile west of here, incidentally, along the riverbank, is the Stephenson family home where George grew up, and it is well worth the detour. It is owned by the National Trust and has been maintained very well, but unfortunately, when I popped along, it was closed to the public.

As the path moved away from the river, we became aware of an old man that was following us. He looked as if he had escaped from an old people's home, and for a minute we considered helping him, as his baggy pants were hanging off him and he looked a bit of a mess. When he started raking around in a bin, though, we decided to leave him alone and moved on.

We had not really stopped all that much today and had not yet had our lunch, so we decided to stop at the next bench for a quick break. Unfortunately, the next bench was a good couple of miles away, and by the time we got there, we were ravenous. It was just a functional stop, as we still had Anthony and those lovely keys to find, and anyway, while we were sat down, an overfriendly sheepdog came over to sniff us and tried to schnaffle our sandwiches.

We moved on and finally caught up with Anthony at the Tyne Riverside Country Park, where we all stopped for well-earned ice cream. It turns out that Anthony had put his phone into airplane mode so he could listen to his music, which he said helped him to walk quicker. No wonder we couldn't catch him, I thought, we didn't have any music.

We were at Newburn, and this place has a small story to tell. There was a battle here, which funnily enough became known as the Battle of Newburn, in 1640.

The Scots came down to take Newcastle, as it was an important port that supplied coal to London. To cut a long story short, the Scots won and even cannily made the English pay them expenses of £850 per day for occupying the north of England. This was one of the battles that led to the English Civil War a year later, although trouble in Ireland was a more significant factor, but one thing leads to another, as they say. It is just a pleasant little park now, although we did see some little kids having what looked like a proper fight, with fists and arms everywhere.

Signs announced the direction of Hadrian's Way, which we presumed was just another name for this walk, and we continued along it, slowly but surely getting to the end, which would not be a minute too soon and would be most welcomed when it finally arrived.

Passing by a slipway, we next came to a

small monument to the Battle of Newburn Ford, as it was apparently called. A little further on, we came across the Tyne Amateur Rowing Club, who had a very impressive clubhouse, and across the river, there was Tyne United Rowing Club, who did not. We imagined a bit of friendly rivalry going on between the two, or maybe even not so friendly. I have never really tried rowing but would love to give it a try, but when I have been on the rowing machines at the gym, which is not all that often, trust me, it nearly killed me, so perhaps I'll give it a miss come to think of it.

After passing under Newburn Bridge, the path took us along what looked like an old railway line, and at the end of that, only a small housing estate stood between us and the A1. Somewhere on our left, although we couldn't see it, was Newburn Church, which is where George Stephenson chose to marry two of his three wives, though not at the same time, I should probably add.

When he was young, George fell in love with a local girl called Betty Hindmarsh, but her dad wouldn't let them marry because George was poor at the time. George, therefore, married Fanny Henderson here in 1802, but when she died, and as he was considerably richer then, Betty's dad finally allowed them to get hitched, the gold digger that he was. George brought Betty here next, and promptly married her, but then inexplicably she died too. Perhaps fearing a curse, George finally chose a different church for his third and final wife, Ellen Gregory, who was actually his housekeeper while he was married to Betty, the sly devil. Betty was probably his one true love, though, as when he popped his clogs, it was her that he chose to be buried with for all eternity.

Newburn also has another famous, and slightly earlier link to railways, which may well have influenced Stephenson. William Hedley was born here, and while you might not have heard of him, you may well have heard of what he built. Puffing Billy was one of the first steam locomotives that actually worked, and was used to haul coal at nearby Wylam Colliery, which is, of course, the village where Stephenson was born and raised.

Luckily there was a bridge over the A1, and after that, it was just a short stroll down a hill to the car which was luckily still there. Less than an hour later, we were back at the campsite and enjoying a barbecue, having showered and changed all in record time. Everyone tucked into the food, with there being more than enough to go around, and after that, we decided to pop to a local pub and treat the ladies to a nice glass of wine.

The Twice Brewed Inn was just a short drive away, funnily enough in the village of Twice Brewed, which was just across the road from Once Brewed. The name relates to the fact that pubs in this area used to sell weak beer, and was intended to tell prospective customers that they will get a proper drink within these walls.

We grabbed ours and went to sit in the

beer garden at the back to enjoy the evening sun, which had paid a surprise visit. It was far from warm, though, and it wasn't long before we came back into the warmth of the pub itself. We found a handbag under the table where we sat, which was promptly handed in at the bar, and we sat for a pleasant half-hour chatting about this and that, and whiling the time away. Happily, the beer wasn't weak at all and went down rather well.

The ladies had spent the day in Carlisle and had visited the castle and the park with the kids, where they had licked the walls and seen the bible with the bullet stuck in it along with much more by the sounds of it, and had quite a nice time by all accounts. They had stopped at Hadrian's Wall on the way back but had not managed to see much of it, so we finished our drinks and decided to go and pay it another visit.

Steel Rigg car park was just a short distance to the north, and as this was a particularly impressive part of the wall, we thought they might quite like to see. We were right, and the kids had a run around and managed to expend a fair bit of energy, and by the time we were heading back to the cars, it was getting dark.

Back at the camp, we sat outside, chatting for a while, careful to keep our noise down this time. Robin had been down to the office earlier and told us that the family that had complained about our noise had pitched up late and had not paid and that Steve the manager suspected that this had been their intention all along. This meant that after we had apologized to the manager this morning, he had paid them a visit and had collected his money. The funny thing is, if they had not complained to us, they would not have ended up paying. Karma is a wonderful thing, don't you think? Luckily, they had now packed up and gone, which hopefully meant we would not be woken up by what sounded like the cries of something being eaten alive later that night.

CHAPTER 7

Newburn to Wallsend

Getting going today took a bit longer than usual. We had to cook for everyone once again, which obviously took longer, and then we also had to pack the tents and gear away, for of course today was to be our final day. It didn't help that it wasn't exactly a dry morning, and no matter what we tried, there was no way we could get the tents dry, so decided to sort that out when we were back at home. We had, at least, had a better night's sleep, however.

Everyone pitched in, though, and by 9 am, we were packed up and ready to hit the road. We would leave the van at the visitor centre at Wallsend that marked the official end of the walk and then drive back to Newburn to begin the walk. We reckoned today would be a shorter walk when compared to the other days, and would also be relatively easy and flat as it followed the banks of the River Tyne mostly, which should make it interesting too.

Parking up at Newburn at the same place we had yesterday, we soon had our packs on and were ready to go, but became momentarily distracted by a child's ride-on tricycle that looked like it had been abandoned hereabouts. The site was on a steep hill, and when Chris saw the toy, thinking it the ideal size for his short height, he jumped on it and had a go. Anthony egged him on and gave him something of a push to get him going, which in hindsight was maybe a bit too powerful. Within a couple of seconds, Chris was hurtling at considerable speed down the hill and towards the dual-carriageway, with the River Tyne beyond that.

We were too busy laughing at Chris to register the imminent danger that he was in, and anyway, he fell off once he had picked up enough speed to make the trike unstable on its tiny wheels. A few feet away, Robin was stood talking to a local family who were out walking their dog, and to say they looked somewhat bemused as an old guy wobbled past them erratically would be something of an understatement. Their dog, which was not on its lead, took off after Chris, which certainly didn't help the situation as it nearly got run over in the process. Steering away from this deadly encounter, the trike lost whatever little stability it had left, and almost in slow motion, it left the ground and somersaulted to a surprisingly swift and very funny halt.

Chris was still tangled around the thing,

giggling uncontrollably as were we all, and the dog had caught up with him by now and was sniffing around this body laid on the floor. With that, it cocked its leg, and well, that is the end of that story.

Figuring we had wasted enough time horsing around, we decided we had better move on. The ladies were taking the children to Whitley Bay today, and we were hoping to meet them sometime around mid to late afternoon at the finish point, where they could watch us walk in, hopefully applauding us as we did so and telling us what an amazing accomplishment it was to have walked across the country once again, and all that.

We were initially going to head east, possibly still on some kind of disused railway line, to a place called Paradise, where we would then join the path that was immediately adjacent to the waterfront. This would then take us around a gentle bend and right into the heart of Newcastle itself, where we would stop for lunch as we passed under its famous bridges. From here, we could then continue through the Saints, which are various districts of Newcastle all named after one saint or another, and around a more bendy bit of the river, before finally passing through the more industrial part of the city which would finally take us to Wallsend, the visitor centre, and whatever was left of Segedunum Fort, the last one on the way.

So, we were off, but we then stopped almost immediately to have a look at a small statue at the bottom of the hill. From a distance, it looked like a statue commemorating the thousands of brave souls that take children on donkey rides along our wonderful beaches at the warmer times of the year. I knew that this was probably not so, but I am just saying what it looked like, which was a man leading a presumably modern pair of children on a walk on the back of a beast. I say modern, because the little girl looked as if she was taking a selfie of herself, and the little boy was disregarding all health and safety and dangling both of his legs off the same side and looked in imminent danger of falling off, had he not been welded on, of course.

The statue is, however, nothing to do with beaches and donkey rides, and a small plaque nearby says it is in remembrance of 38 men and boys who were killed in a disaster at nearby Montagu View Coal Pit in 1925. Called *Yesterday, Today, Forever*, the statue both remembers the past, but also looks forward to a brighter future for this area, and yes, that is indeed a camera in the little girl's hand, and she is indeed taking a picture.

The story of the pit disaster is a sad one. It all began on the morning of 30th March 1925. On that day, there were 148 men and boys down the mine, and two of those men were placing charges in holes they had just drilled. What they did not know, however, was that they had done so right next to an old mine, specifically the Brockwell seam, which was now flooded. The resultant explosion saw millions of gallons of water along with large amounts of methane flood into the mine. Men and boys literally ran for their lives, with the mine now in pitch darkness as the gas had extinguished all of their lights. Some grabbed hold of pit ponies, who are said to be able to sense fresh air and thus led them to safety. It took months to pump out the pit, with some of the bodies not being recovered until January of the following year.

Taking in this sombre tale, it was time to move on. The path led us east for half a mile through a green corridor of trees and chirping birds and brought us out at a noisy and seemingly very busy road that we had to follow for a short while before we doubled back somewhat in order to get to the riverbank itself.

Just behind us was an area known as Benwell, which is an obscure area of housing but is worth a mention nonetheless. Benwell gave to the world a spy who would go on to be exchanged in possibly the most famous prisoner and spy swap the world has ever known, yet he remains almost completely unknown, which is perhaps how the powers that be would want it.

His name, or one of his names anyway though certainly his real name, is William Fisher. He was born in the city in 1903 to his German father and a Russian mother who had emigrated to the city some time previously and was a pretty normal child who went to a good school in Whitley Bay. He must have felt strong links to the motherland, though, as he went there to train as a soldier until the Russians decided that he would be much more valuable in other areas due to his language skills as well as his background in general. During the Second World War, therefore, he fought against the Germans, and as we were all on the same side, this was not technically a problem.

After the war, however, he was recruited by the KGB and sent to America, where he became a proper spy, and a bit of a problem, though his story is truly amazing. He was tasked with re-activating a network of agents whose job was to smuggle atomic secrets out of Los Alamos and back to Russia. No one is quite sure how successful this was, but he was awarded a top Soviet honour, the Order of the Red Banner, around this time, which suggests some success. The Americans, on the other hand, said he achieved nothing substantial, but you would perhaps expect them to say that for strategic reasons and to deter others.

In 1952, Fisher was moved to New York and given a new assistant, Reino Häyhänen, which is when things started to go wrong. Häyhänen was a bit of a character but really tried to immerse himself in American life, chiefly by spending large amounts of official money on booze and prostitutes. He was also extremely inept by any standards, and certainly for the standards expected of a spy. One notorious example is the time he received secret instructions on a piece of microfilm hidden in a hollowed-out nickel. Unfortunately for the lackadaisical Häyhänen, he accidentally used the coin to buy a newspaper, which then spent the next seven months travelling around New York City. One rather surprised newspaper delivery boy came across it at some point though and managed to drop it, splitting it in two and revealing its secret, and immediately handed it in to the authorities.

Fisher notified Moscow that he was encountering severe problems while trying to deal with the complete noodle that they had sent him, so a few weeks later, Häyhänen was recalled to Moscow, when they cunningly sent him a secret message saying that he was being promoted and that he should come back to Moscow real quick, pretty please. Häyhänen wasn't stupid, though, and he instead disappeared with quite a lot of KGB cash and re-emerged in Paris sometime later where he handed himself in to the American Embassy, told them of his KGB connections, and requested asylum. It is probably obvious to most of us that stealing from the KGB is never going to end well, but there you go. Defecting is probably only going to make the situation worse.

Anyway, although they were a bit sceptical at first, when the Americans saw a hollowed-out coin containing a microfilm, they sat up and took notice, and it didn't go unnoticed that this coin was similar to the one found in New York. Ultimately, Häyhänen spilled the beans on more or less everything he knew, and sold-out Fisher big time.

The FBI put Fisher under surveillance, and after a few weeks, they moved in and arrested him. It is at this point that Fisher gave his name as Rudolf Ivanovich Abel, which was actually the name of one of his friends who had died sometime earlier. Fisher reckoned that when his handlers saw Abel's name in the papers, they would immediately know that it was in fact, Fisher.

Convicted of spying, Fisher was sentenced to several decades in prison, but he never co-operated with the Americans, primarily as he wanted to see his family again one day. Lo and behold, he finally got his chance when in 1960 an American spy plane piloted by Francis Gary Powers was shot down over Russia. The Americans thought that their U-2 spy plane flew above the height that any Soviet missile could reach, but, well, guess what? Surprise!

Two years of protracted negotiations resulted in Fisher being sent one way across a bridge in Berlin, while Powers was simultaneously sent the other way, proper spy stuff. Fisher spent the rest of his life in Russia, somewhat disillusioned, and died of lung cancer in 1971. Powers was sacked from his job as a test pilot, although this might be because he wrote a book in which he was not exactly nice about the CIA, which is not advisable when they are your former employer. He too soon died, in a helicopter crash in 1977 while working for a television station as a news pilot. Häyhänen avoided any and all espionage charges and was relocated to New Hampshire where he lived under the protection of the CIA, which of course meant that he, too, would probably soon be dead. He was, in fact, the first to go, when he died in a car accident in Pennsylvania in 1961. I say accident, but I think we all know that it probably wasn't. There is a school of thought that suggests he was assassinated by the KGB, but we will probably never know for sure. If any of this is beginning to sound a bit familiar, this story has recently been told in the movie Bridge of Spies starring Tom Hanks, but I bet you never knew it all started right here, in Newcastle, but enough of that, it's time to move on.

The path along the riverfront was very new and very smart, with finely maintained shrubbery and some kind of rusty metal sculpture greeting us almost immediately. A short while later, a raised wooden decking told us all about the riverfront at Elswick. This place is, for instance, where the vallum reached its easternmost point, although the wall did, of course, continue on to Wallsend.

This area was also the site of a huge factory belonging to William Armstrong, who is an interesting character in himself. Armstrong was a prolific inventor and industrialist born around here in 1910, who became Sir William Armstrong when he turned over all of his gun patents to the government and took nothing in return, well, nothing other than his knighthood. He was an early advocate of renewable energy, and in the mid-1800s he predicted that Britain would turn its back on coal within two centuries and instead adopt both hydro and solar generation, which was a pretty good guess, you have to admit.

He is also the inventor of modern artillery and invented a rifled breech-loading gun after seeing the difficulties of muzzle loading weapons in the Crimean War. This gun was also revolutionary in that it fired a shell as opposed to a ball, which further increased accuracy. The principles of these guns remain valid even in today's modern weapons.

As well as all of the above, Armstrong also built Newcastle's famous swing bridge as well as the mechanism that operates Tower Bridge in London, and he somehow found the time to restore Bamburgh Castle in Northumberland. The really bizarre thing though, is that Armstrong spent sixteen years training as and then working as, wait for it, a solicitor, until he was 37 years old, which is a bit odd, when you think about it, and never formally trained in engineering as such. If you remember rightly, John Clayton trained as a lawyer, but then he too also went on to do something completely different as well.

Lastly, Armstrong also built a very famous house called Cragside, which is unique in that it was the first-ever to be powered by hydro-electricity, which can be found a few miles north of Newcastle at Rothbury. The house is now owned by the National Trust and is well worth a visit, but maybe not today. Armstrong loved that house, and lived there to the grand old age of 90, before popping his clogs in 1900.

On the sign telling me all this, there are a couple of pictures of Armstrong. In one, he is clearly deep in thought, probably thinking of nozzles and power factors and all that crap, and in the other, he looks like a tramp.

Elswick also gave us someone else who is a bit brainy, so I reckon there must be something in the water around here. Peter Higgs was born just around the corner in 1929, and of course is famous for proposing the Higgs Boson particle, which some have called the God particle. Even Stephen Hawking thought that Higgs was pretty clever, which is truly saying something surely, and suggested that he should get a Nobel Prize, which indeed he did. Boffins at the Large Hadron Collider actually claimed to have discovered the particle in 2012, by which time it had also become known as the *goddam particle*, as it was so goddam hard to find. One scientist, experimental physicist Daniel Whiteson, reckoned it would take a bazillion collisions to detect it, which I reckon must be a really big number. He goes on to say that they ran the experiment to find the particle 40 million times a second, all day and all year, so you work it out. What is the particle exactly? Well, it is basically what enables anything to have mass, such as stars, planets, or even that carving of a big willy that we saw back on Hadrian's Wall. So now you know. Amazingly, Higgs was homeschooled, so once again, there must have been something in the water, though I don't think he ever trained as a lawyer.

Moving on, we come across a strange sort of globe structure, where we stop for a quick break. An American approaches us carrying a day pack, and we get talking about the walk. He is doing the full thing, he says, staying at various hotels and guesthouses along the way, and has sensibly decided to have his baggage shipped from place to place, rather than carrying it like a donkey, he adds.

Although he is technically going the wrong way, as all people in the know, like us lot, go west to east, we tell him he is in store for a delightful week. He did comment about the apparent lack of wall so far, but as he has only gone a handful of miles this is only to be expected, we expertly advise.

We tell him to make sure to check out the hidden section of the wall at Heddon-on-the-Wall, as well as the tallest bit at Hare Hill, and advise him of the fact that he doesn't need to pay to get into Housesteads Fort as the path goes straight through it. We feel a bit smug imparting all of our hard-earned knowledge, but we are delighted to do so, and he seems really grateful for the tit-bits. We talk for far too long but enjoy it thoroughly, but after around half an hour, we finally decide we have to move on.

The path offers more of the same, in that it is beautifully manicured with the odd sculpture every now and then, and is shared by cyclists and pedestrians alike. The view to the south is fab, with lots of little apartment blocks over there that must enjoy similarly pleasant vistas.

As we approach what would be the first of Newcastle City Centre's many fine bridges, there is an additional delight visible across the water. This is Dunston Staiths, and would look like a long wooden bridge had it actually crossed the river. It doesn't though, it runs along the southern river-bank for what looks like a very long way, which means we seem to be walking past it for ages and ages.

It is, in fact, supposed to be the largest wooden structure in Europe, and is basically some kind of artificial loading dock where goods from ships could be loaded directly onto trains which were able to come to the very edge of the water on top of this wooden giant. At over a thousand feet long, and with four railway lines atop it, it was opened in 1893 and was in use until the late 1970s.

Unfortunately, arsonists targeted this monolithic giant in 2003 and again in 2019, though there are efforts to raise the money to repair it. You can enjoy a pleasant and pleasurable walk along and around the Staiths if you fancy crossing the river, assuming of course that you're a very, very good swimmer or you don't mind the considerable walk up to the nearest bridge and back again.

That bridge, by the way, is the Redheugh Bridge and is the third that stands on this site. It is clearly very modern, and although it looks very stylish and slender, it was built to withstand being hit by a ship weighing ten thousand tonnes and was opened by none other than Lady Di in 1983.

It replaced a bridge that had stood there for most of the 20th century without incident, which had just reached the end of its life, but the first bridge built here was far more interesting.

That one had been opened in 1871, but by 1885 it had developed major structural faults, though this wasn't in the least bit surprising as it had been built by a guy called Thomas Bouch. As the bridge continued to deteriorate, it became clear that it would be cheaper to rip it down and start again, which is exactly what they did, with the idea that it would be better to pull it down than wait for it to fall down, which is exactly what happened to another bridge that Bouch built.

Bouch was born near Carlisle and gained prominence when he became the first person to successfully design, build and put into practice the world's first roll-on roll-off train ferries, which was actually pretty successful. If he has stuck to that, then all might have been well, but he didn't and turned his hand to bridge building, unfortunately.

Indeed, one of his bridges, the Belah Viaduct, was described by an influential paper as being one of the lightest and cheapest ever, which really should have made people think twice, I reckon.

His claim to fame, though, or perhaps more appropriately infamy, was the Tay Bridge. Opened in June 1879, Queen Victoria herself enjoyed a ride over it and promptly gave Bouch a Knighthood. Unfortunately, just six months later, on 28th December, a train was travelling over the bridge during a storm, which was typical December weather of course for Scotland, when the bridge collapsed and took the train with it, killing 75 people.

A subsequent inquiry found that the bridge had been *badly designed, badly built and badly maintained*, and there is even an example of workers dropping a girder into the water, fishing it out sometime later, and using it anyway.

Immediately after this disaster, Bouch's peers decided to have a bit of a closer look at some of his other work, just in case. His viaduct at South Esk was demolished and replaced, and a pier in Edinburgh, the Portobello Pier was taken down, which proved pretty easy, as it had already started to rust and was pretty much falling into the sea anyway.

Lastly, Bouch had somehow wangled the contract to build the Forth Bridge, a decision which was immediately revoked, with the bridge finally being built by Sir John Fowler and Sir Benjamin Baker, which is perhaps why it still stands to this day, albeit after countless cycles of non-stop painting, and like Hadrian's Wall, is now a UNESCO World Heritage Site.

Newcastle has another bridge worth mentioning of course, and that is the world-famous Tyne Bridge, which is clearly visible ahead of us. You may already know that the Sydney Harbour Bridge, opened in 1932, was based on the Tyne Bridge, which opened in 1928. If you do, then you are wrong, as it is the other way around, you see. How can this be so, I hear you ask? How can the Tyne Bridge be based on the Sydney Harbour Bridge when it was built first? Well, that's simple – it wasn't, well, not technically, anyway. It is just a case that the much bigger Australian bridge took much longer to build. Work down under began in 1923, while it did not get underway up north until 1925, hence making Newcastle the copy cats. The number three seems to be particularly relevant here, in that the Australian bridge is approximately three times higher, longer and wider than its northern cousin, which probably also helps to explain why it took three times longer to build.

I have not been to Australia to see the bridge in Sydney, but I bet it must be a spectacular sight because in my eyes the one in Newcastle is pretty impressive in itself. To exaggerate its size, though, when I took a picture of it, I made sure Chris was in it because as we all should know by now, he is really, really tiny.

Newcastle is famous for many things, and we could spend all day talking about them, but there are a couple of things worth mentioning. Joseph Swan came from here, who invented the incandescent light bulb of course and built it at his factory in Benwell in the city, which probably explains how William Armstrong managed to get hold of them when he lit up Cragside. Before you try to correct me and say that it was Thomas Edison who invented the light bulb, I am afraid I will have to tell you that this is not quite so. Edison did indeed file a patent in 1879 for a working bulb, but Swan had already done this in 1878. There were issues with Swan's design, though, which Edison certainly improved upon. After a bit of a court battle which cost a lot of money and solved nothing, they finally decided it would be cheaper and easier to bang their heads together. Ultimately, they formed Edison-Swan United, which became one of the biggest manufacturers of light bulbs in the world. Bizarrely perhaps, some of their first light bulbs used bamboo for the filament. While this might sound odd, bamboo is nowadays making a bit of a come-back and is seen as an eco-friendly material to make all sorts of stuff. As I sit and write this, I am wearing socks made from bamboo, really, and while I am not actually drinking out of a cup made of bamboo, I do indeed own one.

On another note, Ant and Dec also come from here, which is quite expected, as does Mr Bean, or at least Rowan Atkinson, which was not quite as expected, to be honest. There are countless others, including Chris Donald who founded Viz magazine, which explains a lot surely, but as I said, we could go on all day, so much has this place given the world.

We were right in the heart of the city now, and bustling it was at almost midday. We stopped at the Riverside Pub just next to William Armstrong's swing bridge, which still looks pretty good even after all these years, and sat in the sun watching the world go by. Someone came along and asked us if we wanted to buy a phone, which we didn't, and a couple went past having a heated argument, though about what it was hard to tell.

I was hoping a boat would come along, so we could see the bridge in action, but after half an hour, it was time to move on, and nothing had happened.

On the other side of the river was the church of St Mary's, and next to it was a really weird modern building that looked to my eye like an armadillo. This is the Sage and is a concert venue and music hall. Actually, it is three separate venues, as inside the outer steel and glass shell, there are three distinctly separate buildings. It

has already hosted some top name bands and per-
formers and is generally well-liked, but those who
have a problem with it liken it to a giant slug.
By the way, the other side of the river is technically the completely different town of Gateshead,
which seems a bit odd as they are so close together.

As we continue along the riverbank, there
is still no sign of the wall, and I am beginning to
wonder if we have seen the last of it. This area is
very smart and cosmopolitan nowadays, and this
is in part due to the fact that a fire burned almost
everything down here in 1854. It is known as the
Great Fire of Newcastle and Gateshead, which is
not a very catchy name I have to say.

Anyway, one dark and dreary night in Oc-
tober of that year, a fire began in a mill on the
Gateshead side of the river. Ironically, this mill
had burned down three years earlier and was rebuilt to the exact same design, which was a bit of
a stupid thing to do in retrospect. Regardless, it
burned away quite merrily for some time, with a
large crowd gathering on the Newcastle side of the
river to watch the excitement. Unfortunately, the
mill contained large quantities of wool and oil,
which both burn really well, but when combined,
they produced something resembling napalm.
Even more unfortunately, the fire soon spread to a
warehouse next door, which had among its inventory items such as nitrates, brimstone, manganese
and naptha. To give you an idea of what happened

next, you could use these ingredients to make a bomb.

The large crowd continued to watch the excitement across the river presuming they were safe, but guess what? The explosion was huge, and initially blew down the crowd at the other side, and could be heard as much as 20 miles away in Hartlepool. Next, burning articles including chemicals, linens, and rocks, began to rain down like artillery, injuring and killing many. Fire then took hold in the buildings on the north side, too, which soon consolidated itself in the surrounding area, and in a very short time indeed, both sides of the river were nothing but a blazing inferno.

Dozens died, and bodies could only be identified from personal possessions. The fire took days to put out properly, and the devastation was huge, with much of the city centre gone. A public inquiry could only guess as to the cause of the fire, but in the end, the blame was put on the combination of chemicals that were stored together, and rules were put in place to stop such practices in the future.

On a positive note, the enormous destruction caused by the blaze had at least one beneficial effect. Huge swathes of the city centre were razed to the ground, paving the way for what came next, which was the cosmopolitan area we now found ourselves leisurely wandering through.

We seemed to be leaving the city centre behind and found ourselves walking past a small modern complex with café seating outside. It must have been either incredibly cheap or did very good food, as it was positively rammed. This was the Pitcher & Piano and had we not stopped a little while back, this would have been an excellent place to park bums for a while. Beyond this, there was a model globe, which I presumed was a nod to Newcastle's history as a port.

Almost immediately after passing the globe, our world changed from one of the hustle and bustle and excitement of the city centre to one of quiet suburban solitude, in just a matter of minutes. There were still modern apartment blocks on our side of the river, but the other bank looked almost rural.

We passed a sign that said we had only four miles to go before Wallsend, which meant we were more or less done of course, and I think we were all looking forward to getting to the end of the walk. I had hoped the sign would also have told us how many miles it was to Bowness, but alas, it did not.

We walked along and came to the small River Ouseburn, which we had to cross using the road bridge, before coming back down on to the riverside path. Passing the Cycle Hub, which was a sort of café, sort of shop, communal-style place, we took advantage of possibly the last toilets until the end, before carrying on. Wandering through what seemed to be the world's biggest car park, we were halfway across it when a friendly motorist told us that the car park was a dead end and that we should double back, which saved us a good few minutes at least.

We followed a path along a desolate road that looked as if it, too, would soon become a dead end, but it did not and was where a large truck carrying out a three-point turn failed to see us and came pretty close to making us the dead end. Passing a stark industrial area, we were then surprised to turn in to a pleasant mews, with some very nice, although rather small, houses. Unfortunately, this too proved to be the wrong way, but it only took us a couple of minutes to get back on track, where we found ourselves at the Merchants Tavern Pub, which was on a small and pleasant marina. It was not long before we left all that behind us, where we seemed to be back into the countryside, although, in reality, we were still deep within the city.

We walked around one final bend in the river, appropriately enough named Walker Riverside Park, before the path took us away from the water's edge one last time, and we found ourselves, well, lost. A sign pointed the direction to Hadrian's Wall Walk, although Robin seemed convinced that this was the way we had come. Chris and I looked at each other, shrugged our shoulders, and followed Robin and Anthony on a magical mystery tour through some kind of industrial estate. We voiced loudly several sarcastic statements about missed pages and being lost, but Robin either ignored us or genuinely did not hear us. We could clearly see where we should be, which was on the top of the bank to our left on a path running parallel with ours, so figured we must still be heading in the right direction, however, so it wasn't a major diversion.

I am not sure what business the companies around here were in, but they had some huge, and I mean huge, reels of pipeline or cable, so strongly suspected a nautical theme. We seemed to pass many of them, and after what seemed like a very long walk, although it was probably barely a mile, we found ourselves back on the right path and heading to Wallsend.

We followed this path, and apparently had it to ourselves, and I wondered how long we had left to go. These last miles were ticking down very slowly, and it seemed a lot more than four miles since we had seen the sign for Wallsend, but we carried on anyway. As we left the city of Newcastle boundary, marked by a huge sign at a zebra crossing, we figured we really, really must be nearly there, and we found ourselves struggling, though this was probably psychological.

Whenever we go on a walk, we always feel we have had enough just as we are about to finish. This seems to be the case whether we are out for a short 10 miler, or if we do a mammoth, for us anyway, 25-mile walk. This is exactly how we felt now, and we all felt that we had simply had enough.

We left the path just after the zebra crossing and decided to take the road for the last section, as that way we would also see whatever was left of Segedunum Fort, which was probably going to be not much in all honesty.

Rounding a corner, there was one last point of interest worth mentioning before we get to the fort itself. A large and fancy red-brick building on Neptune Road is the site of one of the very first power stations in the country. Neptune House Power Station was built by Charles Merz and helped this region become one of the major industrial areas in the country by giving businesses access to electricity for the first time ever. Merz was yet another Newcastle native, born here in 1874, and was affectionately known as the Grid King, as it is him that came up with the idea for the power grid as we know it today.

He proposed electric trams and electric trains and even built a hybrid electric tank in the Second World War, so was way ahead of his time. Unfortunately, he was killed by a German bomb in 1940, so that was the end of that.

Just a few hundred feet further on, we finally arrived at Segedunum, and there was, perhaps surprisingly, rather a lot of the fort left. I had presumed, wrongly, that the city would long ago have been built over the site, in the same manner, that it had seemed to have consumed the wall. But a vast open field stood before us, with clear footings and foundations easy to see. Segedunum means strong, and it has certainly stood the test of time. It has also become one of the most excavated forts along the whole of the wall, apparently, although we seem to have heard this quite a lot by now. There is even, to our delight, a small part of the wall still to be seen here, though that is just across the road near some houses, and looks suspiciously new.

We had a look around the site and found to our surprise that there is even a reconstructed bathhouse, though we couldn't get in. After this, we went into the visitor centre itself, where we got our last passport stamp, which obviously signalled the end of our walk, and spent some of our hard-earned money on yet more tat. I got my photo taken with the centurion outside, though I didn't go to the top of the viewing tower as I couldn't be bothered and didn't want to pay the entrance fee for what would probably be a ten-minute look around, as I was aware we had to be meeting the ladies soon.

They do have some good exhibits in there, though, so it might be worth a visit at some point. Although they don't have any Roman penises, they do have a rather interesting Roman toilet seat as well as a handle with the word *virgin* stamped on it, although I believe it is something to do with olive oil.

I later found out that they had Stephenson's Geordie Lamp here, and had I known I would have definitely gone in. This is a miners' safety lamp designed by none other than George Stephenson, the *Father of the Railways*, although he was derided at the time and was even accused of copying the more famous Davy Lamp, invented by Sir Humphry Davy, although this was never so. I had come across this story sometime before, so would just like to have seen it, but never mind.

CHAPTER 8

Conclusion

It occurred to me that the ladies had not been here to meet us as they said they would, and I wondered where they were. I mentioned this to Robin, who decided to ring his wife, at which point a rather heated conversation developed.

Apparently, our female superiors had been given the wrong postcode and were currently sat in their car waiting for us. Unfortunately, they were sat 20 miles to our west, at Heddon-on-the-Wall. We had no idea how this had happened, but we decided to blame Robin regardless, and quite frankly, we found it rather funny.

We arranged to meet them back at our starting point for today, which was back in Scotswood near the little pony statue, which is exactly where we drove to when we jumped into the van a couple of minutes later.

For some unfathomable and strange reason, the ladies were in a bit of a mood with us, but I advised Robin that it was nothing that a bunch of flowers wouldn't fix.

After a few hours in the car, we were all back home in Hull, and as it was the height of summer and we were home at a reasonable hour, we decided to meet up in a local pub later that evening.

We spent the night talking about our week, boring the women with our tall tales of what had happened over the last few days. We told them of the rather unusual and creative carvings along the wall and suggested that they come with us next time and to have a look themselves, but that was clearly never going to happen. We regaled them with stories about the longest bit of the wall and the tallest bit of the wall, about the people we had met along the way and the things we had seen and the food we had eaten, and I have to say they were very polite and never once told us to shut up.

We even bored them with a description of how Hadrian's Wall gave us an answer to that question asked by so many, *What did the Romans ever do for us?* Well, just walk along the wall, and you will see evidence of many things they gave us. Straight roads, obviously, which nowadays help us get to work quicker, so thanks for that. Central heating, which admittedly is pretty useful in the frozen north, as well as language, with many of our modern words based on original Latin, such as the villa in Aston Villa, as well as school, subway, pirate and province, and countless more. They also gave us our calendar and concrete, both of which have had a huge impact on our modern society, and I could not imagine a world without either of these, to be honest, so there you go.

We discussed which walk we could do next, and considered the West Highland Way, which was too far away, and the Pennine Way, which was too long. The Trans-Pennine Trail was a possibility, as was the Viking Way, but we never made a decision that night.

We talked about the sections of this walk where there hadn't been enough wall, or any wall for that matter, both at the beginning and at the end. We discussed the middle bit, where there was lots and lots of wall, but also lots and lots of hills, which had made it a pretty hard, and argued about whether or not the best fort was Birdoswald, Housesteads, or Chesters. Birdoswald was good, Housesteads was impressive, but Chesters, of course, had at least one willy carved into the floor, so we were never going to agree on this.

We all agreed that Bowness seemed so far away and a long time ago, even though it had only been a few days since we had set off, and we talked about the countless interesting things we had seen along the way. The beautiful countryside looking down across the valley of the River Irthing just before Birdoswald had clearly left quite an impression on us all, as had the wildness of the landscape on the central section, particularly Windshields Crags and Highshield Crags. Sycamore Gap had been another high-point that we all agreed on, and I don't think I was the only one who was going to go home and watch Robin Hood once again, probably followed by Braveheart.

We had not had a bad run with the weather, and although we did get quite a lot of rain on one of the days, this is only to be expected in England, and anyway, we had been well prepared.

On a last note, I think my own personal favourite part of this walk had been, without doubt, the section between Birdoswald and Housesteads Forts. The sheer wildness of the landscape, along with the miles and miles of undulating wall snaking its way before us gave me exactly what I had been looking for in this walk, and is the classic section that you would expect the Hadrian's Wall Walk to be.

Add to that Sycamore Gap, and you've got the perfect walk.

AFTERWORD

Thank you for taking the time to read this book. I hope you enjoyed reading it as much as I enjoyed writing it.

I always like to take time to find out about the places that I am walking through as I find it makes for a much more interesting walk. As much as I take time to be as accurate as possible, sometimes history can be a bit vague, and at times downright contradictory.

In that spirit, I take full responsibility for any innacuracies, but if you really feel strongly about something, then please get in touch with me via the contact page on my website at paul-amess.co.uk.

Also on that website are some photos taken from each of my walks, which you are welcome to laugh at.

BOOKS BY THIS AUTHOR

54 Degrees North

Drawing a straight line across England at a latitude of exactly 54 degrees and walking along it as close as he can, join Paul as he sets out to learn about this tiny strip of the country and its rich history including events, people and places. Starting on the east coast in Yorkshire, and somehow ending up in Lancashire, he encounters murderers, film stars, witches and more, all linked in more ways than you might imagine.

Rambling On: Lost On The Cleveland Way

Join Paul as he navigates 109 miles along the Cleveland Way and around the North Yorkshire Moors. Starting in Helmsley on the wettest day of the year, he thinks it can't get worse, but then Storm Francis comes. Accompanied by his good friend Rob, who carries most of the gear and does most of the cooking, they get lost, sunburned, blistered, and blown away. Learn about pirates, inventors and famous people along the way as Paul rambles on in more ways than one, and find out where the unluckiest house in Yorkshire is. And if you want to know what Mick Hucknall has to do with Whitby, and learn about a modern day sailor who stole his own boat, read on. . . .

Coast To Coast: Finding Wainwright's England

Join Paul as he follows in the great Alfred Wainwright's footsteps on one of the world's best known and most popular walks. Taking in beautiful valleys, misty moors, lovely lakes and pleasing plains, find about about the literal and spiritual highs and lows of this 192 mile walk from St Bees to Robin Hood's Bay, all told in a flowing, candid and light-hearted story.

A Walk On The Wild Side

When Paul set out to walk the Wolds Way, he had no idea of the wealth of interesting stories, people, and amazing landscapes he would encounter in what is essentially his own back yard. Following this little gem of a national trail from the shores of the Humber estuary in the middle of winter, up through the dales and valleys of the beautiful Wolds, Paul encounters an ancient land with more history than you can possibly imagine.

Printed in Great Britain
by Amazon